Eat Well Live Well

READER'S DIGEST

Fresh Fish and Seafood

Eat Well Live Well

READER'S DIGEST

Fresh Fish and Seafood

Published by The Reader's Digest Association Limited
London • New York • Sydney • Montreal

FRESH FISH AND SEAFOOD is part of a series of cookery books called
EAT WELL LIVE WELL and was created by Amazon Publishing Limited.

Series Editor *Norma MacMillan*
Volume Editor *Sharon Brown*
Art Director *Ruth Prentice*
Photographic Direction *Ruth Prentice, Alison Shackleton*
DTP *Peter Howard*
Editorial Assistant *Jasmine Brown*
Nutritionists *Jane Griffin, BSc (Nutri.), SRD,
Fiona Hunter, BSc Hons (Nutri.), Dip. Dietetics*

CONTRIBUTORS
Writers *Sara Buenfeld, Carole Clements, Linda Collister,
Beverly LeBlanc, Sara Lewis, Maggie Mayhew,
Kate Moseley, Maggie Pannell, Marlena Spieler, Kate Whiteman*
Recipe Testers *Catherine Atkinson, Bridget Colvin,
Emma-Lee Gow, Clare Lewis, Gina Steer*

Photographers *Martin Brigdale, Gus Filgate, William Lingwood*
Stylist *Helen Trent*
Home Economists *Jules Beresford, Lucy McKelvie, Lucy Miller,
Bridget Sargeson, Linda Tubby, Sunil Vijayakar*

FOR READER'S DIGEST
Project Editor *Rachel Warren Chadd*
Project Art Editor *Louise Turpin*
Production Controllers *Kathy Brown, Jane Holyer*

READER'S DIGEST GENERAL BOOKS
Editorial Director *Cortina Butler*
Art Director *Nick Clark*
Series Editor *Christine Noble*

ISBN 0 276 42474 3

First Edition Copyright © 2001
The Reader's Digest Association Limited
11 Westferry Circus, Canary Wharf, London E14 4HE

Copyright © 2001 Reader's Digest Association Far East Limited
Philippines copyright © 2001 Reader's Digest Association Far East Limited

All rights reserved. No part of this book may be reproduced, stored in a retrieval system or transmitted in any form or by any means, electronic, electrostatic, magnetic tape, mechanical, photocopying, recording or otherwise, without permission in writing from the publishers.

® Reader's Digest, The Digest and the Pegasus logo are registered trademarks of The Reader's Digest Association, Inc, of Pleasantville, New York, USA.

Notes for the reader
• Use all metric or all imperial measures when preparing a recipe, as the two sets of measurements are not exact equivalents.
• Recipes were tested using metric measures and conventional (not fan-assisted) ovens. Medium eggs were used, unless otherwise specified.
• Can sizes are approximate, as weights can vary slightly according to the manufacturer.
• Preparation and cooking times are only intended as a guide.

The nutritional information in this book is for reference only. The editors urge anyone with continuing medical problems or symptoms to consult a doctor.

Contents

6 Introduction
Eating well to live well

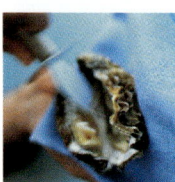

8 Fabulous Fish
10 Fish in a healthy diet
12 Lean and versatile white fish
16 Heart-healthy oily fish
18 Fruits of the sea
22 Preserved fish
24 Cooking fish and shellfish
26 Back to basics

28 Fish First
30 Tomato and crab soup
32 Chinese shrimp soup
34 Chunky fish soup
36 Lobster bisque
38 Seafood choux puffs
40 Parmesan-topped mussels
42 Lemon mackerel pâté
44 Three-fish blinis
46 Gravad lax with ginger
48 Smoked haddock tartlets
50 Thai fish cakes with dipping sauce
52 Salmon and watercress pots
54 Sesame prawn and crab toasts
56 Grilled oysters with fennel and spinach topping

58 For Maximum Vitality

- **60** Crab and avocado salad
- **62** Trio of warm seafood salad
- **64** Lobster salad with lime dressing
- **66** Marinated kipper salad
- **68** Provençal tuna and pepper salad
- **70** Smoked trout and pasta salad
- **72** Grilled salmon salad
- **74** Fennel, apple and herring salad
- **76** Prawn, melon and mango salad

78 Fast Fish

- **80** Griddled halibut steaks with tomato and red pepper salsa
- **82** Chinese-style steamed plaice rolls
- **84** Hake en papillote
- **86** Quick-fried squid with chilli and fresh ginger
- **88** Scampi provençal
- **90** Anchovy and sesame-topped tuna
- **92** Mini fish pizzas
- **94** Stir-fried scallops and prawns
- **96** Classic grilled Dover sole
- **98** Pan-fried swordfish steaks with Mexican salad

100 Main Course Fish

- **102** Spicy grilled sardines
- **104** Herbed fish crumble
- **106** Thai green curry with monkfish
- **108** Cod with spicy Puy lentils
- **110** Smoked haddock kedgeree
- **112** Salmon with tarragon mayonnaise
- **114** Mackerel with gooseberry sauce
- **116** Pesto fish cakes
- **118** Haddock with parsley sauce
- **120** Sole goujons with tartare dip
- **122** Baked trout with cucumber sauce
- **124** Prawn gumbo
- **126** Fish and mushroom pie
- **128** Spaghetti with clams
- **130** Cod with a gremolata crust
- **132** Indian-style fish
- **134** Teriyaki swordfish brochettes

136 Especially Good

- **138** Italian seafood stew
- **140** Baked whole fish with grapefruit
- **142** Salmon koulibiac
- **144** Seafood paella
- **146** Skate with citrus-honey sauce
- **148** Oriental sea bass
- **150** Parma-wrapped lemon sole
- **152** Turbot with sauce maltaise
- **154** Seafood and chive pancakes

- **156** A glossary of nutritional terms
- **159** Index

Eating well to live well

Eating a healthy diet can help you look good, feel great and have lots of energy. Nutrition fads come and go, but the simple keys to eating well remain the same: enjoy a variety of food – no single food contains all the vitamins, minerals, fibre and other essential components you need for health and vitality – and get the balance right by looking at the proportions of the different foods you eat. Add some regular exercise too – at least 30 minutes a day, 3 times a week – and you'll be helping yourself to live well and make the most of your true potential.

Getting it into proportion

Current guidelines are that most people in the UK should eat more starchy foods, more fruit and vegetables, and less fat, meat products and sugary foods. It is almost impossible to give exact amounts that you should eat, as every single person's requirements vary, depending on size, age and the amount of energy expended during the day. However, nutrition experts have suggested an ideal balance of the different foods that provide us with energy (calories) and the nutrients needed for health. The number of daily portions of each of the food groups will vary from person to person – for example, an active teenager might need to eat up to 14 portions of starchy carbohydrates every day, whereas a sedentary adult would only require 6 or 7 portions – but the proportions of the food groups in relation to each other should ideally stay the same.

More detailed explanations of food groups and nutritional terms can be found on pages 156–158, together with brief guidelines on amounts which can be used in conjunction with the nutritional analyses of the recipes. A simple way to get the balance right, however, is to imagine a daily 'plate' divided into the different food groups. On the imaginary 'plate', starchy carbohydrates fill at least one-third of the space, thus constituting the main part of your meals. Fruit and vegetables fill the same amount of space. The remaining third of the 'plate' is divided mainly between protein foods and dairy foods, with just a little space allowed for foods containing fat and sugar. These are the proportions to aim for.

It isn't essential to eat the ideal proportions on the 'plate' at every meal, or even every day – balancing them over a week or two is just as good. The healthiest diet for you and your family is one that is generally balanced and sustainable in the long term.

Our daily plate

Starchy carbohydrate foods: eat 6–14 portions a day

At least 50% of the calories in a healthy diet should come from carbohydrates, and most of that from starchy foods – bread, potatoes and other starchy vegetables, pasta, rice and cereals. For most people in the UK this means doubling current intake. Starchy carbohydrates are the best foods for energy. They also provide protein and essential vitamins and minerals, particularly those from the B group. Eat a variety of starchy foods, choosing wholemeal or wholegrain types whenever possible, because the fibre they contain helps to prevent constipation, bowel disease, heart disease and other health problems.

What is a portion of starchy foods?

Some examples are: 3 tbsp breakfast cereal • 2 tbsp muesli • 1 slice of bread or toast • 1 bread roll, bap or bun • 1 small pitta bread, naan bread or chapatti • 3 crackers or crispbreads • 1 medium-sized potato • 1 medium-sized plantain or small sweet potato • 2 heaped tbsp boiled rice • 2 heaped tbsp boiled pasta.

Fruit and vegetables: eat at least 5 portions a day

Nutrition experts are unanimous that we would all benefit from eating more fruit and vegetables each day – a total of at least 400 g (14 oz) of fruit and vegetables (edible part) is the target. Fruit and vegetables provide vitamin C for immunity and healing, and other 'antioxidant' vitamins and minerals for protection against cardiovascular disease and cancer. They also offer several 'phytochemicals' that help protect against cancer, and B vitamins, especially folate, which is important for women planning a pregnancy, to prevent birth defects. All of these, plus other nutrients, work together to boost well-being.

Antioxidant nutrients (e.g. vitamins C and beta-carotene, which are mainly derived from fruit and vegetables) and vitamin E help to prevent harmful free radicals in the body initiating or accelerating cancer, heart disease, cataracts, arthritis, general ageing, sun damage to skin, and damage to sperm. Free radicals occur naturally as a by-product of normal cell function, but are also caused by pollutants such as tobacco smoke and over-exposure to sunlight.

What is a portion of fruit or vegetables?

Some examples are: 1 medium-sized portion of vegetables or salad • 1 medium-sized piece of fresh fruit • 6 tbsp (about 140 g/5 oz) stewed or canned fruit • 1 small glass (100 ml/3½ fl oz) fruit juice.

Dairy foods: eat 2–3 portions a day

Dairy foods, such as milk, cheese, yogurt and fromage frais, are the best source of calcium for strong bones and teeth, and important for the nervous system. They also provide some protein for growth and repair, vitamin B_{12}, and vitamin A for healthy eyes. They are particularly valuable foods for young children, who need full-fat versions at least up to age 2. Dairy foods are also especially important for adolescent girls to prevent the development of osteoporosis later in life, and for women throughout life generally.

To limit fat intake, wherever possible adults should choose lower-fat dairy foods, such as semi-skimmed milk and low-fat yogurt.

What is a portion of dairy foods?

Some examples are: 1 medium-sized glass (200 ml/7 fl oz) milk • 1 matchbox-sized piece (40 g/1½ oz) Cheddar cheese • 1 small pot of yogurt • 125 g (4½ oz) cottage cheese or fromage frais.

Protein foods: eat 2–4 portions a day
Lean meat, fish, eggs and vegetarian alternatives provide protein for growth and cell repair, as well as iron to prevent anaemia. Meat also provides B vitamins for healthy nerves and digestion, especially vitamin B_{12}, and zinc for growth and healthy bones and skin. Only moderate amounts of these protein-rich foods are required. An adult woman needs about 45 g of protein a day and an adult man 55 g, which constitutes about 11% of a day's calories. This is less than the current average intake. For optimum health, we need to eat some protein every day.

What is a portion of protein-rich food?
Some examples are: 3 slices (85–100 g/3–3½ oz) of roast beef, pork, ham, lamb or chicken • about 100 g (3½ oz) grilled offal • 115–140 g (4–5 oz) cooked fillet of white or oily fish (not fried in batter) • 3 fish fingers • 2 eggs (up to 7 a week) • about 140 g/5 oz baked beans • 60 g (2¼ oz) nuts, peanut butter or other nut products.

Foods containing fat: 1–5 portions a day
Unlike fruit, vegetables and starchy carbohydrates, which can be eaten in abundance, fatty foods should not exceed 33% of the day's calories in a balanced diet, and only 10% of this should be from saturated fat. This quantity of fat may seem a lot, but it isn't – fat contains more than twice as many calories per gram as either carbohydrate or protein.

Overconsumption of fat is a major cause of weight and health problems. A healthy diet must contain a certain amount of fat to provide fat-soluble vitamins and essential fatty acids, needed for the development and function of the brain, eyes and nervous system, but we only need a small amount each day – just 25 g is required, which is much less than we consume in our Western diet. The current recommendations from the Department of Health are a maximum of 71 g fat (of this, 21.5 g saturated) for women each day and 93.5 g fat (28.5 g saturated) for men. The best sources of the essential fatty acids are natural fish oils and pure vegetable oils.

What is a portion of fatty foods?
Some examples are: 1 tsp butter or margarine • 2 tsp low-fat spread • 1 tsp cooking oil • 1 tbsp mayonnaise or vinaigrette (salad dressing) • 1 tbsp cream • 1 individual packet of crisps.

Foods containing sugar: 0–2 portions a day
Although many foods naturally contain sugars (e.g. fruit contains fructose, milk lactose), health experts recommend that we limit 'added' sugars. Added sugars, such as table sugar, provide only calories – they contain no vitamins, minerals or fibre to contribute to health, and it is not necessary to eat them at all. But, as the old adage goes, 'a little of what you fancy does you good' and sugar is no exception. Denial of foods, or using them as rewards or punishment, is not a healthy attitude to eating, and can lead to cravings, binges and yo-yo dieting. Sweet foods are a pleasurable part of a well-balanced diet, but added sugars should account for no more than 11% of the total daily carbohydrate intake.

In assessing how much sugar you consume, don't forget that it is a major ingredient of many processed and ready-prepared foods.

What is a portion of sugary foods?
Some examples are: 3 tsp sugar • 1 heaped tsp jam or honey • 2 biscuits • half a slice of cake • 1 doughnut • 1 Danish pastry • 1 small bar of chocolate • 1 small tube or bag of sweets.

Too salty
Salt (sodium chloride) is essential for a variety of body functions, but we tend to eat too much through consumption of salty processed foods, 'fast' foods and ready-prepared foods, and by adding salt in cooking and at the table. The end result can be rising blood pressure as we get older, which puts us at higher risk of heart disease and stroke. Eating more vegetables and fruit increases potassium intake, which can help to counteract the damaging effects of salt.

Alcohol in a healthy diet
In recent research, moderate drinking of alcohol has been linked with a reduced risk of heart disease and stroke among men and women over 45. However, because of other risks associated with alcohol, particularly in excessive quantities, no doctor would recommend taking up drinking if you are teetotal. The healthiest pattern of drinking is to enjoy small amounts of alcohol with food, to have alcohol-free days and always to avoid getting drunk. A well-balanced diet is vital because nutrients from food (vitamins and minerals) are needed to detoxify the alcohol.

Water – the best choice
Drinking plenty of non-alcoholic liquid each day is an often overlooked part of a well-balanced diet. A minimum of 8 glasses (which is about 2 litres/3½ pints) is the ideal. If possible, these should not all be tea or coffee, as these are stimulants and diuretics, which cause the body to lose liquids, taking with them water-soluble vitamins. Water is the best choice. Other good choices are fruit or herb teas or tisanes, fruit juices – diluted with water, if preferred – or semi-skimmed milk (full-fat milk for very young children). Fizzy sugary or acidic drinks such as cola are more likely to damage tooth enamel than other drinks.

As a guide to the vitamin and mineral content of foods and recipes in the book, we have used the following terms and symbols, based on the percentage of the daily RNI provided by one serving for the average adult man or woman aged 19–49 years (see also pages 156–158):

✓✓✓	or excellent	at least 50% (half)
✓✓	or good	25–50% (one-quarter to one-half)
✓	or useful	10–25% (one-tenth to one-quarter)

Note that recipes contribute other nutrients, but the analyses only include those that provide at least 10% RNI per portion. Vitamins and minerals where deficiencies are rare are not included.

Fabulous Fish

Delicious and full of goodness

FISH IS AN IDEAL FOOD for our busy lives – quick and easy to cook and endlessly versatile. It makes the perfect healthy choice for all kinds of tempting meals, as it is a great source of protein and provides many vitamins and minerals. Oily fish also offer beneficial heart-healthy fats. Shellfish, too, are packed with many essential nutrients, as are fat-free seaweeds and sea vegetables. The wide variety of fish and shellfish – fresh or preserved – can be used to make delicious soups and starters, main-meal salads, or family suppers such as fish pie and fish cakes. Special dishes such as paella and koulibiac are great for entertaining.

Fish in a healthy diet

Full of goodness, with a delicious flavour and texture, fish and other seafood are perfect for all kinds of meals. They're quick to cook, and their versatility means it is easy to incorporate them regularly into a healthy diet.

Why eat fish?

Fish and shellfish are very nutritious foods – full of first-class protein, low in saturated fat but often high in other beneficial fats, and packed with essential vitamins and minerals. Because of these benefits, nutrition experts agree that eating fish 2–3 times a week can be a positive aid to good health.

- Protein is essential to keep our bodies working efficiently and we need to eat protein-rich foods each day. A 140 g (5 oz) portion of cooked white or oily fish provides 55% RNI of protein for adult women and 45% RNI of protein for men.
- White fish offers many of the B-complex vitamins, in particular B_{12} which is vital for growth.
- Oily fish is a source of vitamin D, essential for healthy bones, and of vitamin A for healthy eyes and growth.
- Fish and other seafood supply many important minerals, including phosphorus for healthy bones and teeth; selenium, a powerful antioxidant that protects cells against damage by free radicals; and iodine, an important component of the thyroid hormones which control the rate that food is converted into energy.

Fish can be divided into two groups – white fish and oily fish. The principal difference between them is that in white fish the oil is found mainly in the liver; in oily fish, the oil is distributed throughout the flesh.

White fish for lean protein

White fish has very lean flesh and is low in fat and therefore in calories, making it an ideal food for helping to maintain a healthy weight. It is an important source of good-quality protein, providing similar amounts to lean meat but with lower amounts of fat. The deliciously delicate flavour makes white fish a popular choice with children who also like its texture – unlike meat, which has a fibrous texture, white fish has soft flesh containing little connective tissue, so it is easy to chew.

Oily fish for good fat

All fish is good for you, but oily fish can actually help to improve your health. These fish are a major source of polyunsaturated fatty acids such as omega-3, which can help to prevent arteries clogging and so minimise the risk of strokes and heart attacks. It is no coincidence that the Japanese, whose consumption of fish is the highest in the world, have the lowest incidence of heart disease. The old adage that fish is good for the brain is true, too – omega-3 fatty acids are vital for the development of the brain and can help to prevent cerebral haemorrhages by reducing the risk of blood clotting.

Nutritional differences between types of seafood
(typical values per 100 g/3½ oz raw edible fish)

	white fish	oily fish	shellfish
energy	80 kcals	180 kcals	76 kcals
protein	18.3 g	20.2 g	17.6 g
fat*	0.7 g	11.0 g	0.6 g
polyunsaturates	0.3 g	3.1 g	0.1 g
monounsaturates	0.1 g	4.4 g	0.2 g
saturates	0.1 g	1.9 g	0.1 g
carbohydrate	0.0 g	0.0 g	0.0 g
fibre	0.0 g	0.0 g	0.0 g
sodium	60.0 mg	45.0 mg	190 mg

* The total fat figure includes fatty compounds and other fatty acids in addition to mono and polyunsaturates.

Fish and shellfish can be turned into many delicious and nutritious dishes. Clockwise from top left: Try juicy Prawn, melon and mango salad (see recipe on page 76), Cod with a gremolata crust (see page 130) or moist Lemon mackerel pâté (see page 42)

Put shellfish on the menu now and again

Like fish, shellfish are low in fat, although they contain a higher level of dietary cholesterol. They also contain a high level of sodium. But they offer many essential minerals such as iodine, potassium, iron and zinc. For example, oysters are an excellent source of zinc, and oysters and mussels contain more iron than red meat, when compared weight for weight of the edible part. And shellfish in general are the most reliable natural source of iodine in the normal diet.

An added bonus

Some seafood offers unexpected extra nutritional benefits.
- The canning process softens the bones of fish like sardines, pilchards and salmon and makes them palatable, and eating these bones boosts calcium intake.
- Fish roes provide vitamin C – some types of fish more than others. The fat content of fish fluctuates with the seasons and it is when the female fish are at their fattest, in late summer and early autumn, that they contain large quantities of roe.
- Seaweeds and sea vegetables, widely used in Japanese cookery, are virtually fat-free while offering protein, carbohydrate, and many essential vitamins and minerals.

The future of fish

Fish and shellfish are under constant threat from pollution and over-fishing. Industry effluents, careless sewage disposal and global warming have all played their part in harming the marine eco-system and polluting the world's seas, rivers and lakes. Whether you buy, catch or gather wild fish or shellfish, make sure that they come from unpolluted waters. Most farmed fish and seafood are carefully monitored to eliminate any harmful organisms, but sometimes careless farming can cause diseases in farmed fish. The trend nowadays is towards organic fish farming, which guarantees the fish are fed on only natural foods and are produced in clean, pollution-free waters.

Lean and versatile white fish

For family midweek meals as well as special dishes for dinner parties, white fish is always popular. It can be cooked in so many different ways, and there is an enormous variety of fish to choose from. All are extremely low in fat and high in protein, and also provide some essential vitamins and many minerals.

Lean and lovely

Most white fish fall into two main categories: round and flat. Round fish, such as cod or haddock, have rounded bodies and eyes on either side of the head. They swim with the back fin uppermost. Flat fish, such as plaice or sole, have both eyes on their upper side and the skin there is usually marked as a form of camouflage. Flat fish lead an inactive life on the sea bed, so their flesh has little muscle tone. This makes it delicate and particularly easy to eat and digest.

White fish contain nutritious oils, mainly concentrated in the liver. Some of these – cod and halibut liver oils for example – have long been used as dietary supplements. Fish liver oils contain vitamin A which is essential for healthy vision; vitamin D, essential for growth and the absorption of calcium; vitamin E which works as an antioxidant; and omega-3 fatty acids.

Although fish is a very healthy food, some white fish are short on certain dietary essentials like iron and calcium, and most species contain no vitamin C. So it is a good idea to combine white fish with foods that do provide these nutrients, such as spinach and other iron-rich vegetables; calcium-rich dairy products such as yogurt and milk; and vitamin C-rich vegetables such as broccoli and tomatoes.

An ABC of white fish

The most common white fish are described below. An average portion is 140 g (5 oz), weighed before cooking, without skin and bones. All the healthy cooking methods, such as steaming, poaching and grilling, work well for white fish.

Bream

There are almost 200 different species of bream, of which the best to eat is the gilt-head or dorade – a beautiful fish with dense, juicy white flesh. Bream are usually sold whole or in fillets, and it is essential that their scales be removed before cooking. Sea bream are an excellent source of niacin, a B vitamin involved in the release of energy from food, and of vitamin B_{12}.

Cod

The firm, succulent white flesh of this popular fish becomes deliciously flaky when cooked. Most commonly sold cut into fillets or steaks, cod can also be bought whole and poached or baked. It is an excellent source of iodine, which plays a part in converting food into energy, and a useful source of potassium.

Haddock

This smaller relative of the cod has softer, more delicate flesh. At its best in winter and early spring, when the cold has firmed up the flesh, it is generally sold as fillets, and should be cooked with the skin on. It is an excellent source of iodine and provides useful amounts of potassium and vitamin B_6.

Hake

When very fresh this member of the cod family has firm, lean flesh. It contains few bones and must not be overcooked or it will fall apart. It is usually sold whole or as fillets or steaks. Hake is a good source of phosphorus, which is important for healthy teeth and bones, and a useful source of potassium.

Halibut

Largest of all the flat fish, halibut has dense, meaty flesh that can be dry if not carefully cooked. It is possible to buy whole small fish, known as chicken halibut, but larger fish are usually sold cut into steaks. Halibut is a good source of niacin, and the large roes provide vitamin C.

Hoki

A deep-sea relative of hake, hoki has lean flesh with a flaky texture and rather bland flavour, which is why it is often used in the manufacture of fish fingers. It is always sold as fillets. Hoki is an excellent source of selenium.

John Dory
Although technically a round fish, the body of the John Dory is so slim that it looks almost like a flat fish swimming upright. Its flesh is firm and succulent. John Dory is a good source of phosphorus and a useful source of potassium, which is needed to regulate blood pressure.

Monkfish
This extraordinarily ugly fish has a huge head and a relatively small body. Only the tail is eaten, and it is sold whole or as fillets. The flesh is meaty and firm with a superb flavour. Monkfish is an excellent source of phosphorus and provides useful amounts of potassium.

Mullet
There are 2 types of mullet: red and grey. Red mullet has beautiful reddish-gold skin and lean, firm flesh that tastes a bit like lobster. Being a small fish, it is usually sold whole. The larger grey mullet is a dark silvery colour and has lean, well-flavoured flesh. Grey mullet is sold whole or as fillets, and must be scaled before cooking. The roes, which contain vitamin C, are a delicacy pan-fried and eaten fresh; when dried they are used to make taramasalata. Mullet are excellent sources of selenium and contain useful amounts of potassium.

Plaice
This flat fish has distinctive dark skin spotted with orange. The very soft white flesh can be bland, although it is easy to digest. Sold whole or as fillets, plaice must be very fresh or it will have a woolly texture, and it is best avoided in summer as it is in poor condition after spawning in the spring. Plaice provides many B vitamins – excellent B_{12} and good B_1, B_6 and niacin – and it is a useful source of potassium.

Sea bass
The delicate flesh of this sleek silvery fish has a superb flavour and holds its shape well during cooking. Sold whole or as fillets or steaks, it must be scaled before cooking. Bass is a good source of calcium.

Shark
Shark is a cartilaginous fish (like skate), which means that it has a skeleton composed entirely of cartilage rather than of bones. Its white or pale pink flesh is firm and meaty, and it is always sold skinned and in steaks or fillets. Mako and dogfish (sometimes called huss or rock salmon) are the species most widely available. Shark is an excellent source of selenium and a good source of vitamin A, and unlike most other white fish it contains useful quantities of omega-3 fatty acids.

Skate
Only the 'wings' (actually large, flat pectoral fins) of this cartilaginous fish are generally sold, ready skinned. Skate is best in autumn and winter. Even when very fresh it has an ammoniac smell, but this disappears during cooking. The soft pinkish flesh, which is easily scraped off the cartilage after cooking, has a sweet flavour and its gelatinous quality makes it ideal for fish terrines and mousses. Skate contains excellent levels of vitamin B_{12}, which is vital for the maintenance of a healthy nervous system, and useful amounts of vitamins B_1, B_6 and niacin as well as potassium.

Sole
There are many varieties of these flat fish, including dabs, lemon sole and witch or Torbay sole, but the finest – and most expensive – is Dover sole. This superb fish has firm, juicy flesh with a delicious flavour. Depending on size, sole are sold whole or filleted. They provide useful amounts of vitamin B_{12} and potassium.

Swordfish
This huge game fish has no scales or teeth but a long sword-like nose. Its meaty flesh, usually sold as steaks, can easily dry out, so it is best marinated before cooking. Swordfish is very nutritious, providing excellent amounts of selenium, niacin and vitamin B_{12} as well as useful quantities of potassium.

Tilapia
Sold whole or as fillets, tilapia has lean, moist flesh that contains excellent levels of phosphorus, good amounts of calcium and useful quantities of potassium.

Turbot
The dark, warty flesh of this large flat fish conceals dense, meaty flesh with a wonderful flavour. It is usually sold as fillets. Smaller 'chicken turbot' are sometimes available, and can be cooked whole to serve 4. Turbot is an excellent source of niacin and also offers good amounts of phosphorus and useful quantities of potassium.

Whiting
This fish resembles haddock in appearance. It has soft, bland flesh that can have a woolly texture if the fish is not very fresh. Whiting provides good quantities of selenium and is a useful source of potassium and phosphorus.

Heart-healthy oily fish

All fish are important sources of essential nutrients, but one group – oily fish – is particularly beneficial to health as there is evidence that eating them regularly can help to reduce the risk of strokes and heart disease. Oily fish also offer many of the vitamins and minerals needed for good health and well-being.

Rich and full of flavour

Most oily fish live in shoals near the surface of the sea. They contain more fat than white fish, but it is mainly mono or polyunsaturated fat. They also provide beneficial omega-3 fatty acids, which reduce the tendency of blood to clot, and thus are helpful in the prevention and treatment of heart disease. These healthy fats are stored throughout the bodies of the fish, particularly in the head and muscle tissue. As a further bonus, oily fish offer vitamin A, important for healthy skin and vision; B vitamins, including vitamin B_{12} which is vital for growth; and vitamin D, needed for maintaining strong, healthy bones. Oily fish are rich in minerals too, such as iodine, phosphorus and selenium, as well as calcium if the bones of the fish are eaten.

All oily fish must be eaten when very fresh. They are quick and simple to cook and taste delicious. Their rich-tasting flesh is complemented by sharper flavours such as tart fruit (for example lemon, gooseberries and apple), mustard, pungent spices and herbs such as sorrel.

An ABC of oily fish

The most common oily fish are described below. An average portion is 140 g (5 oz), weighed before cooking, without skin and bones. The best methods for cooking oily fish are grilling, barbecuing and baking.

Anchovy
Usually canned or salted, this small silvery-blue fish is sometimes available fresh, when it can be grilled or pan-fried.

> **Maximising the healthy fats**
>
> Most oily fish do not feed when they are spawning, so during that time they draw their nutrients from the fats stored in their bodies. As a result, the level of fat falls during the spawning season and they are at their leanest just after spawning. For example, herrings have a fat content of about 20% in summer, dropping to only 3–4% in early spring. To benefit fully from the healthy fats contained in oil-rich fish, eat them when they are at their fattest and ready to spawn.

herring and whitebait

anchovies, mackerel and sardines

It may be under 10 cm (4 in) long, but its flesh is packed with flavour, and it provides phosphorus and calcium.

Herring
This sleek silvery fish is not popular with everyone as it contains numerous small bones, but it is very tasty and the nutritious pluses far outweigh this minus point – herring contain large quantities of polyunsaturated fat, excellent levels of vitamin D and useful amounts of vitamin A and potassium. Generally sold whole, herring are at their best when they are really plump and firm, just before spawning. At this stage they are full of roe: females have hard roes and males contain soft roes (milt). Herring roe is a useful source of vitamins A, E and B_1, and contains some vitamin C, so makes a delicious and nutritious snack when pan-fried and served on toast.

Mackerel
This beautiful fish has smooth, steel-blue skin and flesh with a distinctive, rich flavour. It is very nutritious, being an excellent source of iodine, vitamin D and niacin, a good source of vitamins B_2 and B_6, and a useful source of potassium. Mackerel are usually sold whole.

Salmon
Often called 'the king of fish', salmon migrate from the sea into freshwater rivers to spawn. Before spawning, they contain up to 13% unsaturated fat, but by the time they spawn, levels have fallen to about 5%. Wild salmon such as this is at its best in early summer. It contains excellent levels of vitamin B_{12} and useful amounts of potassium.

Salmon is also now raised extensively in fish farms, and this farmed salmon is much less expensive than its wild cousins. Both wild and farmed salmon are sold whole or cut into steaks or fillets.

Sardine
Fresh sardines are delicious, and ideal for grilling and barbecuing. This fish is best in summer, but it is available frozen so can be enjoyed year round. Sardines are an excellent source of selenium and a useful source of potassium.

Trout
There are several varieties of trout, including brown trout and sea trout (also called salmon trout), both of which have a wonderful flavour. The rainbow trout is easy to farm and so is widely available and inexpensive. Trout contain useful amounts of potassium and iodine.

Tuna

This fish can grow to a huge size, so is almost always sold cut into steaks. The dense, meaty flesh varies from pinky-beige to deep red, according to the variety of tuna. It can be dry if overcooked, so is best marinated first. Although lower in healthy fats than other oily fish, tuna is still very nutritious and also contains excellent levels of vitamins B_{12} and D and useful amounts of potassium.

Whitebait
A tiny silvery fish, whitebait is, in fact, young herring or sprats, and so offers the same nutritional benefits as herring. In addition, as it is eaten whole, bones and all, it is a useful source of calcium.

salmon, brown trout and rainbow trout

Fruits of the sea

For a true flavour of the sea, really fresh shellfish cannot be beaten. Low in fat and providing many essential minerals such as iodine, potassium, iron and zinc, shellfish are also quick to cook and extremely versatile.

Crustacean or mollusc?

The seas abound with curious creatures which we loosely call shellfish. There are two main categories of shellfish: 'crustaceans' which have shells and legs and 'molluscs' with shells but no legs.

Like fish, crustaceans and molluscs are low in fat, but unlike fish, they are high in dietary cholesterol. Cholesterol is an essential component of our body structure and a normal constituent of blood, but high levels of cholesterol in the blood are associated with increased risk of coronary heart disease. As a result, for some years shellfish were considered undesirable in a healthy diet. Now scientific research suggests that it is more important to reduce our intake of saturated fat and increase the quantity of foods containing soluble fibre than to avoid eating cholesterol-rich foods. For a small percentage of the population, reducing the amount of dietary cholesterol consumed can help to lower the level of cholesterol in the blood, but for the majority it is the level of saturated fats that is crucial, not the amount of dietary cholesterol.

So as long as shellfish are properly prepared and cooked, we can safely put them back on the menu. It is still important to eat shellfish in moderation, however, as they contain a high level of sodium. On the plus side, shellfish supply many essential minerals and a few vitamins too.

molluscs (clockwise from back left): blue mussels, large or king scallops, queen scallops, oysters, clams, squid bodies, rings and tentacles, and green-lipped mussels

An ABC of shellfish

Shellfish can be cooked in many healthy ways. An average portion (shelled weight of edible flesh) is 100 g (3½ oz).

Clam

This mollusc comes in myriad sizes, from tiny Venus clams to giant specimens. The flesh of most clams has a firm texture and sweet flavour. Clams can be eaten raw, but only if bought from a reputable source. They are an excellent source of phosphorus, which is important for healthy bones and teeth, and a good source of iron.

Crab

There are many different crabs, in all shapes and sizes, from tiny green swimming crabs to huge king crabs with long dangly legs like gigantic spiders. The most familiar in Britain is the common crab, which has brown meat in the body shell and white meat in the claws. The white meat is sweet and succulent with a flaky texture, while the brown meat is rich and creamy. The two can be eaten together or used separately – the brown meat is best mixed with other ingredients to make sauces, soups and so on. Crab is a good source of phosphorus.

Crabsticks are made from crab-flavoured white fish pulp. They are cheaper than fresh crab, but do not really taste like it.

Langoustine

Also known as scampi and Dublin Bay prawn, the langoustine looks like a pale pink miniature lobster. Once caught, the flesh deteriorates rapidly, so langoustines are often cooked and frozen at sea, then sold as frozen scampi tails. Langoustines are a rich source of vitamin E.

Lobster

The king of crustaceans, lobster has firm white meat with an exquisite sweet flavour. It is at its best in summer and autumn, and needs only brief cooking. Lobster contains excellent levels of the antioxidant selenium and useful amounts of iodine and zinc.

Mussel

The beautifully coloured, hinged shell of this mollusc conceals a nugget of sweet, juicy orange flesh. The simplest way to prepare mussels is to steam them open. Be sure to keep the delicious juices from the shells for soups and sauces. Mussels are mineral-rich, providing good quantities of iodine and iron

crustaceans (from left): langoustines, lobster, crab and dressed crab (more iron gram for gram than in red meat) and useful levels of calcium, phosphorus and zinc.

Oyster

Regarded as one of the ultimate luxury foods, oysters are traditionally eaten raw, with a few drops of lemon juice or Tabasco sauce to enhance their iodised flavour. They can also be lightly grilled, poached or steamed, but must not be overcooked or they will become rubbery. Oysters are one of the richest sources of zinc, a mineral needed for reproduction, which may be why they have a reputation for being an aphrodisiac. They also provide excellent amounts of iron and useful levels of potassium.

Prawn and shrimp

The different names given to these tasty crustaceans are only an indication of size – commercially, any prawn measuring less than about 5 cm (2 in) is known as a shrimp. Different species of prawns are found throughout the world and, generally speaking, those from cold waters have the best flavour. If possible, buy prawns in the shell as they will taste better than those sold ready-shelled. Prawns are an excellent source of vitamin B_{12} and a useful source of calcium.

Scallop

For sheer beauty, the scallop is hard to beat, with its elegant fan-shaped shell. Inside, the thick disc of sweet white meat is attached to a vibrant orange, crescent-shaped roe or 'coral', which tastes as delicate and delicious as the white meat. Large or king scallops are sold both in and out of the shell. The small queen scallops are almost always sold shelled. Scallops are an excellent source of selenium and vitamin B_{12} and a useful source of phosphorus and potassium.

Squid

The squid is a cephalopod, a mollusc whose 'shell' has developed inside the body. Sold whole or as rings or tubes, squid requires either very brief or very long, slow cooking – anything in between makes it tough and rubbery. It is an excellent source of vitamin B_{12}.

prawns and shrimps (clockwise from back left): raw king prawns, cooked Mediterranean prawns (in shell and peeled), raw tiger prawns (in shell and peeled), peeled cooked brown shrimps, peeled cooked rose shrimps, and cooked Atlantic prawns (peeled and in shell)

Vegetables from the sea

From a nutritional point of view, seaweeds and sea vegetables are superfoods as they contain protein, carbohydrate and essential vitamins and minerals and they are virtually fat-free.

Beside the seaside
The Japanese have been eating seaweeds and sea vegetables (which grow near the salty shore) for thousands of years, and there has also been a long tradition of eating seaweed in Ireland and Wales. Elsewhere, the health-giving properties of these foods are just beginning to be appreciated. Edible seaweeds are sold in a variety of forms – fresh, dried, pickled in vinegar or flaked as a flavouring – and they can be found in large supermarkets, healthfood shops and speciality food shops. Some can be eaten raw or lightly blanched. All seaweeds are high in sodium, but they are also an excellent source of iodine, and the iodine flavour harmonises wonderfully well with fish and other seafood. Many seaweeds provide vitamin B_{12}.

Carrageen or Irish moss A fan-shaped seaweed from Ireland, this is reputed to be an excellent cure for coughs and colds when boiled and mixed with honey and lemon juice. In common with other seaweeds like agar-agar, carrageen has good gelling properties and is used as a vegetarian gelatine substitute to make jellies and mousses. Carrageen is a useful source of calcium.

Dulse Also called dillisk, this seaweed is popular in Ireland, where it is dried and chewed as a nutritious salty snack or added to soups to make a tasty sea-flavoured broth. Dulse can also be eaten fresh and is delicious cooked and spooned over buttered boiled new potatoes.

Nori and laver Anyone who has eaten sushi will be familiar with nori, the dark brownish seaweed that is dried and pressed into thin sheets to make sushi wrappers. Nori can also be eaten as it is, dipped in soy sauce, or toasted and shredded to be sprinkled over fish or vegetables as a garnish. Laver is the Welsh equivalent of nori. It is boiled to make a thick purée called laverbread, which is coated with oatmeal and fried, or spread on toast or oatcakes for breakfast. Both nori and laver are excellent sources of calcium, potassium and vitamin A.

Wakame Usually sold dried, this Japanese seaweed is an excellent source of calcium, phosphorus, magnesium and iodine. **Kombu** and **hijiki** are other seaweeds used in Japan.

Seashore feasts
Sea vegetables growing by the seashore contain all the goodness of seaweed. Steamed or quickly blanched and tossed in a little butter or lemon juice, they make the most delectable alternative to green vegetables.

Samphire Rock samphire, also called sea asparagus because of its appearance and texture, is at its best in spring and early summer, when its vibrant green shoots are young and tender. Samphire can also be bought pickled, but it has a completely different taste from fresh samphire and the pickling process changes it to greyish-green. Marsh samphire or glasswort is similar to rock samphire and can be eaten in a salad, cooked or pickled. It makes a good accompaniment for fish.

Seakale This cousin of the common cabbage can be tough, but if drifting sand covers the young shoots, shielding them from the light, the resulting yellowish stems will be pale and tender. They make a great alternative to asparagus and can be cooked in the same way. Seakale is a good source of vitamin C.

clockwise from top left: sheets of nori, wakame, samphire and laverbread

fabulous fish

21

Preserved fish

Canning, smoking, drying, pickling and freezing are all good ways of preserving fish so it can be enjoyed year round. Most preserving methods are healthy and lock in all the goodness of fresh fish and seafood so that even those who live miles from the sea can savour its flavour and enjoy its benefits.

Canned goodness

Cans of fish are a very useful part of a well-stocked storecupboard. Oily fish like sardines, salmon and tuna are favourites and these fish retain their vitamin and mineral content when canned. Other ideal standbys are some of the more seasonal shellfish such as mussels, oysters and clams, all perfect for perking up fish pies and pasta sauces.

- Anchovy fillets have a high sodium content, but a little goes a long way and it takes only a small amount to add real flavour to fish dishes. Anchovies can also enhance the flavour of many non-fish dishes, including roast lamb, without making them taste fishy.
- Canned salmon comes in different grades, with the wild Alaskan red salmon having the best flavour. The canning process seals in all of salmon's natural beneficial oils and softens the bones to provide an extra source of calcium if they are eaten. Canned salmon makes a delicious healthy sandwich filling when partnered with watercress. It is also ideal for fish cakes and mousses.
- Sardines were the first fish ever to be canned and are among the most successful. Like salmon, if you eat the bones you will be adding valuable calcium to your diet. For one of the quickest and healthiest snacks possible, drain a can of sardines, mash them with a little lemon juice and serve on wholemeal toast.
- Pilchards are very similar to sardines although slightly larger. They have a coarser flavour but are equally nutritious.
- Tuna is a healthy fish that responds well to canning, and it is preserved in oil, brine or spring water. Tuna is perfect for sandwiches and substantial salads.

Frozen for freshness

Many fish and shellfish are caught far out at sea, days or weeks away from land. To prevent deterioration, they are processed and frozen immediately on the fishing boats. This type of commercial freezing at very low temperatures preserves all the nutrients and ensures that the fish remains ultra-fresh. Frozen fillets and steaks are pre-packed and ready to cook, a wonderful convenience for busy cooks who may not have a fishmonger nearby but wish to include fish regularly in their diet. Other convenient frozen seafood includes shell-on or peeled prawns and mixtures that include mussels, prawns and squid.

The smoking story

There are two kinds of smoked fish: hot-smoked and cold-smoked. In hot-smoking, the fish is given an initial blast of hot air and then slowly cured in the smoke from a hot wood chip or sawdust fire. This cooks it too, so it is bought ready to eat. In cold-smoking, the fish is often salted or brined before curing over the smoke from a slow-burning wood fire. Some cold-smoked fish are eaten raw, while others need to be cooked further. Smoking, whether hot or cold, doesn't destroy the nutrients in the fish.

- Cod and haddock fillets are cold-smoked. When buying, look for the natural pale golden undyed fillets as they have a better flavour than the bright yellow fish which contains artificial colouring. Arbroath smokies are small whole hot-smoked haddock.
- Herrings are cold-smoked to become kippers and bloaters, or hot-smoked to become sprats and buckling. Like their fresh counterpart, they contain high levels of omega-3 fatty acids, which help to protect against stroke and heart disease.

smoked fish (clockwise from top left): smoked trout, peppered smoked mackerel, smoked Finnan haddock, Arbroath smokie, kipper, smoked cod fillet, hot-smoked salmon and cold-smoked salmon

- Hot-smoking mackerel preserves all the nutritious oils and enhances its rich flavour. Smoked mackerel needs no cooking and can be eaten as part of a salad.
- Smoked salmon is usually produced by lightly salting the filleted fish and cold-smoking it, but it can also be hot-smoked which gives it a smoky, roasted flavour. Scottish smoked salmon is generally acknowledged to be the finest of all, but Irish salmon is also superb. Wild salmon has a gamier flavour and drier texture than farmed salmon. Smoked salmon from Canada and Norway is usually cheaper than British salmon and tends to be paler in colour with a lighter flavour.
- Hot-smoked rainbow trout is delicious in salads and sandwiches, or as a first course with bread and salad leaves.

In a pickle

Oily fish are well suited to pickling and can be preserved in flavoured vinegar or brine, or in a dry salt and spice mixture. Pickled fish are low in calories and high in flavour but may also be high in sodium, so should be eaten only occasionally.
- Gravad lax is fresh salmon 'dry' pickled with salt, crushed peppercorns and fresh dill. The process preserves all the goodness of salmon and the fish has a superb texture and flavour. Serve it sliced, with a dill and mustard sauce.
- Marinating herring fillets in vinegar with onions and spices preserves them in the same way that cooking does. Pickled herrings are also available in a sour cream sauce. Rollmops are herring fillets rolled around peppercorns and onions and bottled with hot spiced vinegar.

Ancient methods of drying and salting

Air-drying is a natural process that removes moisture from food, preserving it and concentrating the flavour. Salting is another ancient way of extracting moisture. Both are well suited to fish and their roe. Dried and salted fish have been a staple food in many countries throughout the world for centuries, providing protein throughout the year.
- Dried, salted cod is known as stockfish in Scandinavia, *bacalhau* in Portugal and *baccala* in Italy. It looks like dried shoe leather, but after long soaking in many changes of water, it reverts to its original texture. The soaking process reduces the high sodium content. Poached or baked with tomatoes, onions and garlic, salt cod makes a tasty dish.
- Caviar is the salted roe of the sturgeon. It is available in grains or pressed and the grandest version is beluga. Caviar is low in fat with a moderate protein content, although as with other fish roes, it has high levels of cholesterol and sodium.
- Lumpfish roe, which can be black or orange, is a cheaper alternative to caviar as is the bright orange or red salmon roe.
- The hard roes of cod and grey mullet are salted, dried and pressed. They are often used for the Greek dip taramasalata.

pickled, dried and salted fish (clockwise from left): dried salted cod, dried salted cod's roe, rollmops, marinated herring fillets, Bismarck herrings, salmon roe, gravad lax and black lumpfish roe

Cooking fish and shellfish

Fish and shellfish require very little preparation and they positively benefit from a brief cooking time – healthy cooking methods like poaching, grilling, steaming and microwaving are perfect for their delicate flesh. They are extremely versatile too, so you can create a host of nutritious and tempting dishes in next to no time.

For fish, simplest is best

Fish does not need elaborate cooking. In fact, its delicate texture benefits from the fastest and simplest cooking methods to retain its natural juices and fresh clean taste. Some very fresh fish like salmon are sometimes simply marinated in citrus juice or other acidic liquid. This turns the flesh of the fish opaque and adds a tangy flavour, while retaining the valuable nutrients of the fish.

Unlike meat, fish has naturally tender flesh so it is always better to undercook rather than overcook it. Fish is ready if the flesh is still very slightly translucent when eased away from the bone, or flakes easily when tested with the point of a sharp knife or skewer. Alternatively, you can test by pressing the prongs of a fork into the thickest part of the fish; they should go in easily, just meeting a slight resistance near the bone.

Since most fish comes from the sea, it already has a natural salty taste so it needs little or no added salt.

Baking fish in a parcel keeps it beautifully moist. Here a whole sea bass is baked with Oriental flavours (see recipe on page 148)

Fish cooking know-how

• Cooking fish in parcels ensures the flesh stays moist and the fish cooks in its own juices. Whole fish can be stuffed with herbs or vegetables, then wrapped in foil or put in a baking dish and covered tightly, then baked in the oven at 180°C (350°F, gas mark 4). Allow about 10 minutes per 450 g (1 lb). Thick fillets or steaks can be parcelled up in baking parchment or foil with vegetables and herbs, moistened with wine or lemon juice and baked *en papillote*.

• Oily fish such as herrings, mackerel and trout are delicious grilled, and their own healthy oils can do all the basting. White fish should be marinated first or covered with a glaze or coating to protect its delicate flesh. Depending on size and thickness, fish will take 4–12 minutes to cook.

• Barbecuing is a tasty way to cook fish. Try whole oily fish like sardines, trout or mackerel and cook for 4–8 minutes on each side, depending on the size of the fish. If you use a special fish grill that holds whole fish, it will be easy to turn them over. White fish is best marinated if it is to be cooked straight on the barbecue, or it can be wrapped in foil parcels with herbs and lemon juice. Or cut chunky white fish into cubes and thread on skewers with vegetables to make wonderful kebabs. Be sure to oil the barbecue grid to ensure the fish doesn't stick to it.

• Fish can make a delicious and easy dish when braised with vegetables and a little fish stock or wine. As fish needs so little cooking, it is best to soften the chopped vegetables in a flameproof casserole first, then lay the fish on top and braise on the hob or in the oven. Allow 7–8 minutes for fillets and steaks or about 20 minutes for a whole 1 kg (2¼ lb) fish.

• Microwaving is an excellent way to cook fish, ensuring that it retains all its moistness, natural flavour and nutrients, and it takes only a few minutes. When microwaving fish fillets or

Quick steaming is the traditional way to cook mussels. Instructions are in the recipe on page 38, step 3

Cooking crustaceans and molluscs

- When cooking a live crustacean, such as a lobster or crab, first wrap it in a damp tea towel and put it in the freezer for 1–2 hours to make it comatose. Then plunge it into a large saucepan of boiling water and quickly clamp on the lid. For crab, cook for 10–12 minutes, whatever its size; lobsters need about 15 minutes for the first 450 g (1 lb) and then 10 minutes for each subsequent 450 g (1 lb).
- Prawns and shrimps can be poached, pan-fried, grilled, barbecued or stir-fried. Raw prawns only take a few minutes to change to a bright pink colour, which indicates they are done. Keep the cooking of ready-cooked prawns very brief so that they are just heated through.
- Molluscs such as mussels and clams are usually steamed open, whereas oysters and scallops are more often prised open. Whether steamed, grilled, stir-fried or sautéed, cooking should be brief as overcooking will make the shellfish tough.

steaks, add a little stock or lemon juice and cover with kitchen paper. If you are microwaving whole fish, slash the skin a few times to prevent it from bursting.
- Poaching fish brings out its flavour and keeps it very moist. Fish stock, water and wine, or milk can all be used for poaching. The liquid will retain the water-soluble vitamins from the fish, so don't throw it away – use it to make a sauce or soup. When poaching fish, the liquid should never boil – it should be just under simmering point. For a whole fish (around 3.5 kg/6½ lb), put it into a pan with cold liquid to cover, put the lid on and bring to a simmer. Poach for 8–12 minutes, then remove from the heat and cool in the liquid.
- Steaming is one of the healthiest ways to cook fish as it uses no fat and, because the fish does not come into direct contact with liquid, most of the vital nutrients are retained. Use herbs and aromatics to add flavour, or steam fish on a bed of seaweed or samphire for an extra taste of the sea.
- Fish is delicious briefly pan-fried in a little oil or butter. If you use a non-stick frying pan or a ridged cast iron grill pan and heat the pan well, you'll need only a tiny amount of fat. Pan-fried fish takes only 2–3 minutes cooking on each side, depending on the thickness of the fish.
- Stir-frying is ideal for small pieces of fish, which take only moments to cook.

Beyond the fish finger

Fish is an ideal food for children but many are reluctant to try it. Encourage them to eat more fish by tempting them with colourful dishes like chunky kebabs with cherry tomatoes and courgettes, stir-fries or pasta dishes with fish, sweetcorn and peas. Form fish cakes into fishy shapes, or serve in burger buns with tomato ketchup. Or try sole goujons (see page 120) and chunky oven chips (see Some More Ideas, page 116), shown below, served with a green vegetable. Skinless, boneless white fish makes a good addition to a toddler's diet as it has a delicate flavour and is easy to digest. Mash it with potato or carrot, stir tiny pieces into small pasta shapes or purée it into soup.

fabulous fish

Back to basics

Nothing can beat the flavour of fish and shellfish, but they must be carefully prepared and stored to ensure that you enjoy them at their beneficial best. Always eat fresh shellfish and oily fish on the day it is bought.

Buying seafood

The best place to buy fresh fish and shellfish is from a trusted fishmonger, but they are becoming rare. Larger supermarkets now have excellent wet fish counters, and there are also mobile fish vans that travel around some parts of the country selling fresh seafood. Wherever you buy fish, always follow these guidelines.

- Really fresh fish do not smell fishy but give off an aroma of seaweed and the sea. When buying whole fish, check that the skin has a metallic shine and is covered in clear slime. The scales should be plentiful and firmly attached; stale fish shed their scales. The flesh should be firm and springy and the gills should be a vibrant red or deep pink; do not buy fish with brown or greyish gills. The eyes should be clear and slightly protruding; avoid fish with dull, sunken eyes.
- Testing pre-packed fish for freshness is more difficult, since you cannot smell it. For fish portions, check that the flesh is firm and moist, with a pearly translucency, and that any visible skin is shiny and bright. Buy from a reputable source that has a quick turnover.
- The flesh of all shellfish deteriorates rapidly and can become poisonous, so it is essential to buy only the very freshest. Seafood that is past its best has an unpleasant ammoniac or fishy odour. Crustaceans such as prawns and shrimps should have crisp, firm shells and should smell very fresh. On no account buy them if they smell of ammonia – a sure indication that they are stale.
- When buying molluscs, such as oysters, mussels or clams, always check with the fishmonger that they have come from 'clean' waters.
- It is sometimes more convenient to buy frozen seafood. Obviously, you cannot apply the smell and feel tests, but do make sure the packaging is undamaged, and that there is no visible ice inside it and no sign of freezer burn or any discoloration. Frozen prawns and shrimps and seafood mixtures should still be solidly frozen in their bags; do not buy them if they have started to thaw.

Freezing and thawing rules

When buying fresh fish, always ask the fishmonger if the fish has been previously frozen. Packaged fresh fish often has a label stating whether it has been frozen – if it has not, then ask. Basically, if the fish you are buying has been previously frozen then you must not re-freeze it as the texture will be ruined and harmful bacteria could cause food poisoning. However, it is fine to use this fish in cooked dishes like fish pies or lasagnes and then freeze the cooked dish. If absolutely necessary, you can freeze fresh (previously not frozen) white fish at home. To preserve the delicate texture, wrap the fish tightly in foil and freeze at the lowest possible temperature, preferably on fast-freeze. Once frozen, white fish can be stored for up to 3 months at -18ºC (- 4ºF). Oily fish like herrings and mackerel do not freeze successfully as their oils cause them to spoil rapidly.

Fish should be thawed as slowly as possible to preserve the flavour and texture. Place in a dish, cover and leave overnight in the fridge, or thaw in the microwave on the defrost setting. Take care not to over-thaw it or it will dry out. Once thawed, pour off any liquid (you can use it in a nutritious soup or sauce), pat the fish dry with kitchen paper and cook it as soon as possible.

It is not advisable to freeze raw shellfish at home. Ready-frozen shellfish can be stored in a home freezer for 2 months.

Storing fresh seafood

- Ideally, fresh fish should be eaten on the day of purchase, but this is not always practical. As soon as you get it home, remove the packaging and wipe the fish with a clean damp

cloth. Place it on a plate, cover with cling film and store at the bottom of the fridge for no more than 24 hours.
• Live crustaceans, such as crabs or lobsters, should always be cooked on the day of purchase. If you cannot cook them immediately, wrap in wet newspaper or cover with a very damp tea towel and keep in the coldest part of the fridge.
• Live molluscs, such as mussels, clams, scallops and oysters, should also be eaten on the day you buy them. Put them in a large container, cover with a damp cloth and keep in the coldest part of the refrigerator until ready to cook. Oysters should be stored cupped side down to keep them fresh in the juices contained in the shell. Never store live molluscs in fresh unsalted water or they will die.

Safe handling
• Always use an immaculately clean, separate chopping board to prepare fresh fish and shellfish so that any harmful bacteria that might be present are not transferred to other foods. Wash your hands thoroughly before and after handling the fish.

• Make sure that fish fillets are free of small bones that might get stuck in the throat. Run your fingertips over the cut side of the fish to feel for bones and use clean tweezers to pluck out any that you find.
• The edible parts of a crab are the white meat in the claws and the creamy-brown meat in the body shell. When the crab's body has been separated from its hard shell, discard the greyish-white stomach sac and the feathery gills (dead men's fingers) as these are inedible.
• When taking lobster meat from the shell, discard the sac between the eyes in the head, the dark intestinal vein that runs down the tail and the grey spongy, feathery gills. The red coral or roe and the creamy greenish-grey liver (called the tomalley) can both be eaten.
• Before cooking mussels they should be well scrubbed and the wiry 'beards' removed. If any shells are slightly open, tap them sharply. If they do not close immediately, discard them. After cooking, discard any mussels with closed shells.

Fish stock

A good home-made fish stock can enhance all kinds of fish dishes and it's very simple to make. Use fish trimmings – the head, skin and bones – from any white fish with a good flavour, such as sole, cod or plaice. (Oily fish are not suitable for making stock as they would give it a strong fatty flavour.) Once cooled, the stock will keep in the fridge for 1–2 days or it can be frozen for up to 1 month.

Makes about 1.2 litres (2 pints)
900 g (2 lb) trimmings from white fish, including skin, bones, and heads without gills
1 onion, thinly sliced
4 sprigs of parsley
2 bay leaves
2 carrots, thinly sliced
2 celery sticks, thinly sliced
4 black peppercorns
1.3 litres (2¼ pints) boiling water

Preparation time: 10 minutes, plus 10 minutes cooling
Cooking time: 35 minutes

1 Rinse the fish bones and heads well, then place in a large saucepan. Add the onion, parsley, bay leaves, carrots, celery and peppercorns, and pour in the boiling water. Bring back to the boil, then reduce the heat and simmer gently for about 30 minutes, skimming off the froth and sediment from the surface as it appears.
2 Remove from the heat and leave to cool for 10 minutes, then strain the stock through a fine sieve into a heatproof bowl. Discard the fish trimmings and vegetables. Use the stock at once or cool and chill.

Some more ideas
• For special-occasion fish dishes, use 300 ml (10 fl oz) white wine and 1 litre (1¾ pints) water.
• Use 400 g (14 oz) inexpensive white fish fillet, such as pollock, instead of the trimmings.
• Make a shellfish stock using prawn, crab, lobster or mussel shells instead of the white fish trimmings.

Fish First

Tasty and nutritious soups and starters

FISH AND SHELLFISH make truly delicious soups that are as good for you as they are good to eat, served either to start a meal or as a light lunch or supper dish. Why not try chunky haddock and vegetable soup, or aromatic Chinese mushroom and shrimp soup with noodles? For a special occasion, there's a creamy lobster bisque to savour. Seafood is always a tempting first course. Enjoy favourite starters with a new twist, such as lemon mackerel pâté or gravad lax with ginger and lemongrass. Or experiment with the contemporary flavours of Thai fish cakes, lightly grilled oysters topped with fennel and spinach, or saffron choux puffs filled with mussels and scallops.

Tomato and crab soup

Forget about fiddly and time-consuming crab preparation. Just buy a ready-prepared fresh crab, presented in the body shell, and make this quick and easy soup that captures all the flavours of the sea. Serve it as a starter for 4, or as a light lunch dish for 2, with toasted ciabatta or Granary bread for dunking.

Serves 4
- 15 g (½ oz) butter
- 2 tsp extra virgin olive oil
- 1 large onion, finely chopped
- 400 g (14 oz) potatoes, peeled and finely diced
- 340 g (12 oz) ripe tomatoes, skinned, seeded and diced
- 2 anchovy fillets, drained and chopped
- 600 ml (1 pint) fish stock, preferably home-made (see page 27)
- 200 ml (7 fl oz) dry white wine
- 1 tbsp tomato purée
- 200 g (7 oz) fresh crab meat (brown and white)
- 150 ml (5 fl oz) semi-skimmed milk
- salt and pepper

To garnish
- 3 tbsp soured cream
- 2 anchovy fillets, drained and cut into thin strips
- paprika

Preparation time: 15 minutes
Cooking time: about 30 minutes

1. Heat the butter and oil in a large saucepan. Add the onion and potatoes and cook over a moderate heat, stirring, for 5 minutes or until the onion is softened.

2. Stir in the tomatoes and chopped anchovies, then add the stock, wine and tomato purée. Season with salt and pepper to taste. Bring to the boil, then cover and simmer for 15 minutes, stirring occasionally.

3. Add half of the white crab meat and all the brown meat to the pan and stir in the milk. Cover again and simmer gently for 10 minutes.

4. Ladle the soup into soup bowls and swirl the soured cream over the top. Garnish with the remaining white crab meat, strips of anchovy and a sprinkling of paprika. Serve hot.

Some more ideas
- For a smooth texture, at the end of step 3, purée the soup in a blender or food processor. Stir in an extra 200 ml (7 fl oz) stock or milk, or a mixture of the two, and heat through.
- For a crab and celeriac chowder, replace the onion with 300 g (10½ oz) celeriac, finely diced, and 140 g (5 oz) sliced leek.
- To make an easy storecupboard soup, use a can of white crab meat, about 170 g, well drained, and a can of dressed crab, about 43 g, instead of the fresh crab.

Plus points
- Crab belongs to the same family as the lobster and shrimp, but unlike them, the crab's very small tail is tucked underneath its body. It is a good source of copper, essential in the formation of collagen, a fundamental protein in bones, skin and connective tissue.
- Tomatoes supply appreciable amounts of beta-carotene and vitamin C, both of which have important antioxidant properties. The red colour of tomatoes comes from lycopene, another powerful antioxidant, which research indicates may help to reduce the risk of cancer if included in the diet regularly.
- Paprika comes from a variety of small sweet red pepper. Although only used in small amounts as a spice, it has a particularly high carotene content, and this will add to the antioxidant properties of a dish.

Each serving provides
kcal 265, **protein** 9 g, **fat** 10 g (of which saturated fat 4.5 g), **carbohydrate** 28 g (of which sugars 10 g), **fibre** 3 g

✓✓✓	B_1, B_6, niacin
✓✓	A, C, copper, potassium
✓	B_2, B_{12}, E, folate, calcium, iron, zinc

Chinese shrimp soup

This light, refreshing soup has flavours that are characteristic of Chinese cookery: sesame, ginger and star anise. The dried mushrooms and dried shrimps can be found in larger supermarkets and Oriental food stores.

Serves 4

Shrimp stock
25 g (scant 1 oz) dried shrimps
2.5 cm (1 in) piece fresh root ginger, sliced
4 spring onions
1 whole star anise

Soup
6 dried Chinese mushrooms, about 15 g (½ oz) in total
1 tsp toasted sesame oil
2.5 cm (1 in) piece fresh root ginger, finely chopped
2 spring onions, thinly sliced
55 g (2 oz) bamboo shoots, cut into fine matchsticks
125 g (4½ oz) cooked peeled shrimps or prawns
2 tbsp light soy sauce
1 tbsp fish sauce
85 g (3 oz) fine Chinese egg noodles
fresh coriander leaves to garnish

Preparation time: 1¼ hours
Cooking time: about 10 minutes

1. Put all the ingredients for the stock in a large saucepan with 1.4 litres (2½ pints) water – there's no need to peel or chop the ginger and spring onions as they will be discarded after cooking. Bring to the boil, skimming off any scum, then cover and simmer for 1 hour. Strain the stock and discard the flavourings.

2. While the stock is simmering, rinse the dried mushrooms in cold water and put them in a bowl. Pour over boiling water to cover and leave to soak for 20 minutes. Drain, then discard the tough stalks and cut the mushroom caps into thin slices.

3. Heat the sesame oil in a large saucepan, add the ginger and cook for 30 seconds, stirring. Add the shrimp stock and mushrooms, bring to the boil and simmer for 3 minutes. Add the spring onions, bamboo shoots, shrimps or prawns, and soy and fish sauces. Bring back to the boil, then add the noodles and simmer for 2–3 minutes or until softened. Serve hot, sprinkled with coriander leaves.

Some more ideas

- For a tasty variation, cook fish balls in the stock. To make the fish balls, put 150 g (5½ oz) skinless cod or haddock fillet in a blender or food processor with 1 spring onion, chopped, 1 cm (½ in) piece fresh root ginger, chopped, 1 tbsp beaten egg and 1 tbsp cornflour, and process until smooth. Chill the mixture while making the shrimp stock and soaking the mushrooms. Roll the fish mixture into 16 small balls. In step 3, omit the cooked shrimps or prawns and drop the fish balls into the boiling stock when you add the noodles. Cook for 2–3 minutes or until the balls float to the surface. Add 45 g (1½ oz) baby spinach leaves and bring back to the boil. Serve with shredded coriander leaves scattered over the top.

- The soup can also be served as a light lunch dish. Simply add double the quantity of egg noodles (170 g/6 oz) and shrimps or prawns (250 g/9 oz).

Each serving provides

kcal 166, **protein** 15 g, **fat** 3.5 g (of which saturated fat 1 g), **carbohydrate** 19.5 g (of which sugars 1 g), **fibre** 1 g

✓✓✓	B_1, niacin, copper
✓✓	B_{12}, calcium, iron, selenium
✓	B_6, potassium, zinc

Plus points

- The variety of ingredients used in this tasty soup provides lots of essential nutrients, but the result is still very low in calories.
- Shrimps and prawns are a good source of calcium, an essential mineral for healthy bones and teeth.
- For centuries, ginger has been recognised as having medicinal properties, particularly aiding digestion and preventing nausea. Ginger biscuits are often recommended to pregnant women to help relieve the symptoms of morning sickness.

Chunky fish soup

Even though this soup contains bacon and root vegetables, it has a delicate flavour that makes it an appealing first course at any time of the year. Rich in B-complex vitamins, it is also low in fat and contains a good amount of fibre. Serve with crusty wholemeal or wholegrain rolls.

Serves 4
pinch of saffron threads
2 tsp extra virgin olive oil
55 g (2 oz) lean smoked back bacon rashers, rinded and chopped
85 g (3 oz) waxy potatoes, such as Charlotte, scrubbed and finely diced
85 g (3 oz) parsnips, finely diced
2 celery sticks, finely chopped
85 g (3 oz) onion, finely chopped
1 bay leaf
1 strip of finely pared lemon zest
750 ml (1¼ pints) fish stock, preferably home-made (see page 27)
250 g (8½ oz) skinless haddock fillet, cut into bite-sized pieces
salt and pepper
4 spring onions, finely chopped, to garnish

Preparation time: 15 minutes
Cooking time: about 20 minutes

1. Put the saffron threads in a small frying pan over a moderate heat and stir until they just begin to give off their aroma. Immediately tip the saffron threads onto a small plate and set aside.

2. Heat the oil in a large non-stick saucepan, add the bacon and cook over a moderate heat, stirring, for about 2 minutes. Add the potatoes, parsnips, celery and onion, and cook gently for about 1 minute, stirring frequently.

3. Add the saffron threads, bay leaf and lemon zest, and season with salt and pepper to taste. Pour in the stock and slowly bring to the boil. Reduce the heat to moderately low, half cover the pan and simmer, stirring occasionally, for about 8 minutes or until the vegetables are almost tender when pierced with the tip of a knife.

4. Lay the pieces of haddock on top of the vegetables. Reduce the heat to low and cover the pan tightly. Simmer for 7–8 minutes or until the fish will flake easily and all the vegetables are tender. Remove and discard the bay leaf and lemon zest.

5. Ladle the soup into bowls, sprinkle with the chopped spring onions and serve immediately.

Plus points
- White fish such as haddock is an important source of good-quality protein. On a weight for weight basis, white fish provides similar amounts of protein to that found in lean meat.
- Potatoes do not have as much vitamin C as some other vegetables, but they are an important source because of the large quantity normally eaten.
- Celery was originally grown as a medicinal herb, only being used as a cooked vegetable and salad ingredient in the late 17th century. Green celery contains beta-carotene, which the body converts into vitamin A.

Each serving provides
kcal 148, **protein** 16 g, **fat** 5 g (of which saturated fat 1 g), **carbohydrate** 11 g (of which sugars 4 g), **fibre** 3 g

✓✓✓	B_1, B_6, niacin
✓✓	selenium
✓	B_{12}, C, folate, potassium

Some more ideas

- For a thicker soup, use floury potatoes such as King Edward or Maris Piper. They will fall apart as they cook and thicken the soup.
- Vary the vegetables to use what is in season. Green beans are an excellent alternative to the celery, and turnips can replace the parsnips. Other suitable vegetables include carrots, courgettes, fennel and peppers.
- Monkfish and cod also work well in this recipe. Or try a combination of undyed smoked haddock and fresh haddock.
- Stir 100 g (3½ oz) cooked brown rice into the soup at the end of step 3.
- To turn this into a main-dish soup, increase the amount of vegetables to 200 g (7 oz) each, use 1 tbsp extra virgin olive oil and increase the amount of fish to 500 g (1 lb 2 oz).

Lobster bisque

This recipe makes the most of a lobster – it even uses the shell – so it is a good way to stretch a luxury ingredient. The soup tastes very rich but only uses a small amount of cream – the creamy smooth texture comes from the rice. Serve as a special first course, with slices of warm ciabatta or other bread.

Serves 4

1 small cooked lobster, about 400 g (14 oz)
30 g (1 oz) butter
1 large onion, finely chopped
1 leek, finely chopped
1 carrot, finely chopped
1 celery stick, finely chopped
90 ml (3 fl oz) dry white wine or dry vermouth
1 bay leaf
50 g (1¾ oz) long-grain rice
250 g (8½ oz) plum tomatoes, skinned, seeded and chopped
1 tbsp lemon juice, or to taste
2 tbsp single cream
few drops of Tabasco sauce to taste
salt and pepper
1½ tbsp snipped fresh chives to garnish

Preparation time: 45 minutes
Cooking time: about 40 minutes

Each serving provides

kcal 202, **protein** 8 g, **fat** 8.5 g (of which saturated fat 5 g), **carbohydrate** 21 g (of which sugars 8 g), **fibre** 3 g

✓✓✓	B_1, B_6, niacin
✓✓	A, C, copper, selenium
✓	B_{12}, E, folate, iron, potassium, zinc

1 Pull and twist off the lobster claws and set aside. With a sharp knife cut the body in half lengthways, from tail end through the head. Scoop out the creamy greenish-grey liver (tomalley) and, if it is a female lobster, the red-orange coral or roe. Reserve these together, covered and chilled. Remove the lobster meat from the claws and body/tail shell. Discard all the inedible parts (see page 27). Cut the meat into bite-sized pieces and set aside. Chop the shell into large pieces.

2 Melt 15 g (½ oz) of the butter in a large saucepan over a moderate heat. Add the pieces of lobster shell and sauté until brown bits begin to stick on the bottom of the pan. Add about one-third of the onion, leek, carrot and celery, and cook, stirring constantly, for 1 minute. Add the wine or vermouth and let it bubble for 1 minute. Pour in 1 litre (1¾ pints) water, add the bay leaf and bring to the boil. Reduce the heat and simmer gently for 30 minutes. Strain the lobster stock through a fine sieve, discarding the shell and vegetables, and spoon off any fat.

3 Melt the remaining 15 g (½ oz) butter in a large saucepan over a moderate heat. Add the remaining onion, leek, carrot and celery. Cover and cook, stirring frequently, for about 5 minutes or until the vegetables are soft and just starting to colour. Stir in the rice. Add the tomatoes and lobster stock and bring almost to a boil. Reduce the heat, cover again and simmer for about 25 minutes or until the rice and vegetables are very tender.

4 Add the tomalley to the soup with any coral, pressing them through a sieve if any pieces of lobster shell are evident. Purée the soup with a hand blender, or in a food processor or blender, until very smooth.

5 Return the soup to the saucepan if necessary and set over a moderately low heat. Add the lemon juice and simmer gently for 2–3 minutes or until heated through. Stir in the cream, season with salt and pepper to taste, and add a few drops of Tabasco sauce. Ladle the soup into warm bowls, add the reserved lobster meat and garnish with the chives.

Plus points
- Plain boiled lobster is healthily low in saturated fat. It is the addition of large amounts of high-fat foods such as butter, cream and mayonnaise that makes many classic lobster dishes so rich.

Some more ideas

• For a hearty chowder-like soup to serve 6, in step 5 add 2 courgettes, finely diced, 225 g (8 oz) frozen sweetcorn kernels, 1 large potato, peeled and finely diced, and 3 plum tomatoes, skinned, seeded and diced, with the lemon juice. Simmer, covered, for 15–20 minutes or until all the vegetables are tender.

• If no lobster shell is available to make the stock, you can use 1 litre (1¾ pints) fish stock, preferably home-made (see page 27), instead. To give the bisque extra flavour and colour, steep a pinch of saffron threads in 4 tbsp hot water for 10 minutes, and add with the fish stock and tomatoes in step 3.

Seafood choux puffs

These golden mini choux puffs are filled with mussels and scallops in a saffron and chive sauce. Both the puffs and filling can be prepared earlier in the day and reheated just before serving.

Serves 6

Choux puffs
55 g (2 oz) butter
75 g (2½ oz) plain flour, sifted
2 eggs, beaten

Mussel and scallop filling
1 small onion, finely chopped
150 ml (5 fl oz) dry white wine
150 ml (5 fl oz) fish stock, preferably home-made (see page 27), or water
large pinch of saffron threads
pared zest and juice of ½ lemon
500 g (1 lb 2 oz) mussels, scrubbed and beards removed
4 scallops, about 200 g (7 oz) in total
4 tsp cornflour
150 ml (5 fl oz) semi-skimmed milk
2 tbsp snipped fresh chives
85 g (3 oz) rocket leaves
salt and pepper
fresh chives to garnish

Preparation and cooking time: 1½ hours

Each serving provides
kcal 377, **protein** 26 g, **fat** 17 g (of which saturated fat 9 g), **carbohydrate** 26 g (of which sugars 3.5 g), **fibre** 1 g

✓✓✓	B_1, B_{12}, niacin, selenium
✓✓	A, iron, zinc
✓	B_2, B_6, E, folate, calcium, copper, potassium

1. Preheat the oven to 220°C (425°F, gas mark 7). To make the choux puffs, put the butter and 150 ml (5 fl oz) water into a small saucepan. Heat gently until the butter has melted, then bring to the boil. Quickly tip in the flour and beat until the mixture forms a ball. Remove from the heat and leave to cool for 2 minutes, then gradually beat in the eggs to make a smooth paste.

2. Spoon the paste into 18 small mounds, well spaced apart, on lightly greased baking sheets. Bake for 15–20 minutes or until well risen and the tops are crisp. Pierce each choux puff with a small knife or skewer to allow the steam to escape, then return them to the oven for 2–3 minutes to dry out. Set aside until ready to serve.

3. To make the filling, put the onion, wine, stock or water, saffron, lemon zest and seasoning to taste into a medium-sized saucepan and bring to the boil. Add the mussels, cover tightly and cook gently for 5 minutes or until the mussel shells have opened. Discard any mussels that are still shut.

4. Take the pan off the heat and lift the mussels out of the cooking liquid with a draining spoon. Using a fork, take the mussels out of the shells and reserve.

5. Cut the corals off the scallops and reserve. Add the white scallop meat to the mussel cooking liquid, cover and cook for 2 minutes. Add the corals and cook for a further 1 minute. Lift the scallops and corals out of the liquid with a draining spoon, chop and reserve. Boil the cooking liquid until reduced by one-third. Strain and return to the pan.

6. Mix the cornflour to a smooth paste with a little of the milk, then add to the cooking liquid with the remaining milk. Bring the sauce to the boil, stirring until thickened. Stir in the mussels, scallops and corals, and chives. Season with salt and pepper to taste. Heat through gently. (If making ahead, cool and chill, then reheat gently for serving.)

7. If you want to serve the choux puffs hot, reheat in a preheated 180°C (350°F, gas mark 4) oven for 5 minutes. Slit open the choux puffs and spoon in the filling. Arrange on serving plates. Toss the rocket with the lemon juice and pile next to the puffs. Garnish with chives and serve.

Plus points
- Thickening with cornflour is a lower-fat alternative to a butter and flour roux.
- Scallops are an excellent source of selenium, a powerful antioxidant that protects the body against disease.

Some more ideas

• For a drinks party, use the choux paste to make 28 tiny bite-sized puffs, and finely dice the mussels and scallops for the filling.

• If you want to plan ahead, open-freeze the uncooked choux mounds on a baking sheet, then pack into a plastic box. To serve, return to the baking sheet to thaw for 1 hour at room temperature, then bake as in the main recipe.

• For a light lunch for 4, make a choux ring filled with salmon and watercress. Spoon the choux paste into a 20 cm (8 in) ring on a lightly greased baking sheet and bake for 20–25 minutes or until well risen. Slit open the ring horizontally and return to the oven for 3 minutes to dry out. For the filling, poach 450 g (1 lb) salmon fillet in the wine and saffron mixture for 5 minutes, then leave to stand, off the heat, for 5 minutes to complete the cooking. Lift out the fish and flake, discarding the skin and any bones. Boil the poaching liquid to reduce to 120 ml (4 fl oz), strain and use to make the sauce as in the main recipe. Stir in the salmon, the juice of ½ lemon and 20 g (¾ oz) chopped watercress, and heat gently for 2 minutes. Spoon the mixture into the choux ring and fill the centre with more watercress.

Parmesan-topped mussels

Make this stylish starter when you can buy large mussels, such as the green-lipped mussels from New Zealand, as smaller ones can toughen when grilled. Although you only need 24 mussels for this recipe, buy at least 30 because some might have to be discarded. Serve the mussels with chunks of French bread.

Serves 4

100 ml (3½ fl oz) white wine or fish stock, preferably home-made (see page 27)
1 large onion, very finely chopped
3 large garlic cloves, crushed
about 30 large mussels, scrubbed and beards removed
50 g (1¾ oz) fresh wholemeal bread
30 g (1 oz) parsley, chopped
30 g (1 oz) Parmesan cheese, freshly grated
½ tbsp finely grated lemon zest
pinch of cayenne pepper
1 tbsp extra virgin olive oil
lemon wedges to serve

Preparation and cooking time: 30 minutes

Each serving provides
kcal 167, **protein** 12 g, **fat** 7 g (of which saturated fat 2 g), **carbohydrate** 12 g (of which sugars 4 g), **fibre** 2 g

✓✓✓	B_1, B_6, B_{12}, niacin, iron
✓✓	selenium
✓	A, C, folate, calcium, copper, potassium, zinc

1. Pour the wine or stock into a large saucepan, add the onion and garlic, and bring to the boil over a high heat. Boil rapidly for 1 minute. Add the mussels, cover the pan tightly and cook for 2–3 minutes, shaking the pan occasionally. Uncover the pan and give the mussels a good stir. Using tongs, remove the mussels from the pan as soon as they open and set them aside. Discard any mussels that remain shut.

2. When the mussels are cool enough to handle, remove and discard the top shell. Place 24 mussels on the half shell in a single layer in a shallow flameproof dish, loosening the mussels from the shells but leaving them in place. Set the dish aside.

3. Preheat the grill to high. Put the bread in a food processor or blender and process to fine crumbs. Add the parsley, Parmesan, lemon zest, cayenne pepper and olive oil, and process again until well blended.

4. Using your fingers, put a mound of the cheese and crumb mixture on each mussel and pack it down firmly so the mussel is completely covered. Put the dish under the grill and cook for 2–3 minutes or until the crumb topping is crisp and lightly browned. Divide the mussels among individual plates and serve with lemon wedges.

Another idea
- Rather than grilling the mussels with the crumb and Parmesan topping, serve them French-style, cooked in cider. Put 1 litre (1¾ pints) dry cider in the pan with the onion and garlic and boil until reduced to 600 ml (1 pint). Stir in the parsley, lemon zest and cayenne pepper. Add the mussels and steam them open. Transfer the mussels to serving bowls. Season the cooking liquid to taste and ladle it over the mussels.

Plus points
- Mussels are a good source of iron, an essential component of haemoglobin in red blood cells responsible for transporting oxygen around the body.
- Parmesan cheese is a very hard cheese made from unpasteurised skimmed cow's milk. Although Parmesan has a high fat content, it also has a strong flavour and a little goes a long way in a recipe.
- Cayenne pepper, made from one of the smallest and hottest chillies, is often used in herbal medicine to stimulate the circulation.

Lemon mackerel pâté

Whether you are planning a simple family meal or an elegant dinner party, this fresh-tasting smoked fish pâté makes the perfect light starter, served with slices of Granary toast. For an extra special presentation, spoon it into scooped-out lemon shells, which will also enhance the tangy lemon flavour.

Serves 4
2 smoked mackerel fillets, about 125 g (4½ oz) each, skinned
200 g (7 oz) fromage frais
finely grated zest and juice of 1 small lemon
2 tsp bottled soft green peppercorns, drained, rinsed and chopped, or 1 tsp dried green peppercorns, coarsely crushed
1 tbsp finely snipped fresh chives
1 tbsp finely chopped parsley

To serve
sprigs of parsley
lemon wedges

Preparation time: 10–15 minutes, plus 30 minutes chilling

1 Using a fork, break up the mackerel fillets into large pieces and place in a bowl. Add the fromage frais, lemon zest, half of the lemon juice, the peppercorns, chives and parsley. Mash all the ingredients together with a fork. This will make a coarse-textured pâté. For a smooth version, combine the ingredients in a food processor and process. Taste the pâté and stir in more lemon juice if necessary.

2 Spoon the pâté into 4 ramekins, cover with cling film and chill for 30 minutes. Just before serving, top each with a sprig of parsley and serve with lemon wedges.

Some more ideas
• For a smoked trout pâté, substitute smoked trout fillets for the mackerel and add 1 tbsp creamed horseradish instead of the green peppercorns.
• Add a crushed garlic clove and use fresh dill instead of chives.
• Toast 50 g (1¾ oz) shelled walnuts or hazelnuts, chop coarsely and fold into the finished pâté. Season with freshly ground black pepper or a small pinch of cayenne pepper.
• Chill the pâté in a bowl, then scoop out using an ice cream scoop or a spoon and serve in cup-shaped lettuce leaves. Offer crudités for dipping (such as celery, fennel and carrot sticks, strips of red pepper and whole radishes).

• To make lemon shells, cut a sliver off the stalk end of 4 lemons so they stand firmly upright. Cut off a lid from each lemon, about 1 cm (½ in) from the top. Using a grapefruit knife or pointed teaspoon, remove all the flesh from the lemons (keep it for another recipe). Fill the lemon shells with the mackerel pâté and top with the lids. Alternatively, cut the lemons in half horizontally, from the stalk end to the tip. Scoop out the flesh from the halves and fill with the pâté. Serve 2 halves per person.

Each serving provides
kcal 250, **protein** 16 g, **fat** 19 g (of which saturated fat 4 g), **carbohydrate** 3.5 g (of which sugars 3.5 g), **fibre** 0 g

✓✓✓	B_1, B_6, B_{12}, niacin
✓✓	selenium
✓	B_2, iron

Plus points
• Mackerel is an excellent source of vitamin D. Most people obtain all the vitamin D they need from the action of sunlight on skin, but those who remain indoors a lot would benefit from including this fish in their diet on a regular basis.
• Lemons, like other citrus fruits, contain excellent levels of vitamin C. Towards the end of the 18th century, lemon juice was used as a means of protecting sailors against scurvy, the disease caused by vitamin C deficiency.

Three-fish blinis

Blinis are small light pancakes, originally from Russia. The version here is made with wholemeal flour, and the blinis are topped with soured cream, pickled herring, smoked salmon and lumpfish roe. A very special starter.

Serves 6

Blinis
140 g (5 oz) wholemeal flour
1 sachet easy-blend dried yeast, about 7 g
¼ tsp salt
1 tsp caster sugar
175 ml (6 fl oz) lukewarm water
1 egg, separated
175 ml (6 fl oz) lukewarm semi-skimmed milk
1 tbsp melted butter

Toppings
120 ml (4 fl oz) soured cream, well chilled
1 jar black lumpfish roe, about 50 g
150 g (5½ oz) ready-prepared pickled herring, drained
75 g (2½ oz) smoked salmon trimmings
fresh chives to garnish
lemon wedges to serve

Preparation and cooking time: 45 minutes, plus 1½–2½ hours rising time

Each serving provides
kcal 365, protein 22 g, fat 18 g (of which saturated fat 7 g), carbohydrate 31 g (of which sugars 9 g), fibre 3 g

✓✓✓	B_1, B_6, niacin
✓✓	A, B_{12}, folate, copper, iron, selenium
✓	B_2, E, calcium, potassium, zinc

1 Combine the flour, yeast, salt and sugar in a large mixing bowl. Make a well in the centre and add the lukewarm water and the egg yolk. Whisk the water and yolk together, then gradually work in the flour to make a very thick, smooth batter. Cover the bowl with cling film and leave in a warm place, such as an airing cupboard, for 1–1½ hours or until doubled in volume.

2 Whisk the lukewarm milk into the batter to give a mixture with the consistency of double cream. Cover again with cling film and leave in a warm place for ½–1 hour or until there are small bubbles on the surface.

3 Meanwhile, prepare the toppings. Stir the soured cream until very smooth. Carefully separate the lumpfish roe to make it easy to spoon. Using kitchen scissors, cut the pickled herring and smoked salmon into strips about 1 cm (½ in) across and 4 cm (1½ in) long. Cover the toppings and chill until ready to serve.

4 When ready to cook the blinis, preheat the oven to 150ºC (300ºF, gas mark 2). Whisk the egg white until it forms stiff peaks, then gently fold into the batter.

5 Heat a heavy, non-stick frying pan until it is moderately hot, then add a little of the melted butter and swirl it around to coat the pan. Spoon in about 2–3 tbsp of the batter to make a pancake about 7.5 cm (3 in) across. Cook over a moderate heat for 2 minutes or until the surface of the blini is covered in small bubbles and has set. Using a palette knife, turn the blini over and cook the other side for about 2 minutes or until golden brown. Keep the blinis warm, lightly covered, in the oven while cooking the remainder – there will be enough batter to make 18 blinis.

6 To serve, put a teaspoon of soured cream in the centre of each blini, then top 6 with the black lumpfish roe, 6 with pickled herring and the remaining 6 with strips of smoked salmon. Arrange the blinis on a large serving platter, scatter over some chives and serve with lemon wedges.

Plus points
- Wholemeal flour is made by milling the whole grain, including the outer layers of bran and wheatgerm. These layers are good sources of dietary fibre, minerals such as iron and zinc, and B vitamins.
- Soured cream is made by adding a souring culture to homogenised single cream. It has the same fat content as single cream and contains more calcium than double, whipping or clotted cream.

Some more ideas

- For authentic Russian blinis, replace the wholemeal flour with buckwheat flour, a fine speckled flour with a distinctive earthy flavour.
- Home-made pickled kippers are fairly simple to prepare and make a tasty topping for the blinis (this makes enough for 12 blinis). Choose 2 undyed, oak-smoked filleted kippers. Using kitchen scissors, snip each kipper in half along its length. Using a small sharp knife, carefully skin the fillets by placing the knife horizontally between the flesh and the skin and gently cutting the fillets free. Cut the fillets on the diagonal into pieces about 1 cm (½ in) across. For the marinade, mix together 3 tbsp lemon juice, 1 tbsp extra virgin olive oil, ½ small mild onion, thinly sliced, 2 tsp chopped parsley and black pepper to taste. Toss the kipper pieces in the marinade, then cover and chill for several hours or overnight. Drain well before using to top the blinis.

Gravad lax with ginger

The traditional Scandinavian recipe of marinated raw salmon served with a mustard and dill sauce is here given a modern twist, with fresh ginger and lemongrass added to the marinade. Be sure to use really fresh salmon as it needs to be marinated for 2 days. Serve as a starter with slices of wholemeal or rye bread.

Serves 4

225 g (8 oz) piece of very fresh salmon fillet (tail end)

Marinade

1 tbsp coarse sea salt

2 tsp caster sugar

1 tsp mixed black, green and red peppercorns, crushed

15 g (½ oz) piece fresh root ginger, chopped

1 stalk lemongrass, finely chopped

3 tbsp chopped fresh dill

Mustard and dill sauce

3 tbsp mayonnaise

3 tbsp plain low-fat yogurt

2 tbsp Dijon mustard

1 tbsp chopped fresh dill

To serve

1 small avocado

55 g (2 oz) mixed salad leaves

1 cucumber, halved and sliced

½ small red onion, thinly sliced

Preparation time: 20 minutes, plus 2 days marinating

Each serving provides

kcal 278, **protein** 15 g, **fat** 21 g (of which saturated fat 3.5 g), **carbohydrate** 8 g (of which sugars 7 g), **fibre** 1 g

✓✓✓ B_1, B_6, B_{12}, niacin

✓✓ E

✓ A, calcium, iron, potassium, selenium

1 Mix together all the marinade ingredients. Sprinkle half of the mixture over the bottom of a shallow, non-metallic dish. Lay the salmon on top, skin side down, and sprinkle over the remaining marinade, pressing the mixture well into the salmon flesh. Cover the salmon with cling film and place a board and a heavy weight on top. Leave to marinate in the fridge for about 48 hours, turning the fish every 12 hours.

2 When the salmon is ready to serve, prepare the mustard and dill sauce. Combine all the ingredients, stirring well to mix smoothly, and spoon into a serving bowl.

3 Slice the salmon very thinly, cutting diagonally off the skin, so that each slice is edged with a little of the dill marinade. Arrange the salmon on serving plates.

4 Peel and stone the avocado and cut into chunky pieces. Arrange with the salad leaves and cucumber next to the salmon. Sprinkle over the sliced onion and serve with the mustard and dill sauce.

Some more ideas

- For a quicker version of this dish, use 200 g (7 oz) sliced smoked salmon, spreading it out in a shallow dish. To make the marinade, roughly chop the ginger, put it in a garlic press and squeeze the ginger juice over the slices of salmon with the juice of ½ lemon. Scatter over the finely chopped lemongrass and dill, and leave in the fridge for several hours or overnight for the flavours to mingle.
- Make the sauce with crème fraîche (reduced-fat if you like) or soured cream instead of the mayonnaise and yogurt combination.

Plus points

- Avocados do contain large amounts of fat; however, most of the fat is unsaturated and this can help to protect against heart disease. Fully ripe avocados mashed with some lemon juice make a good healthy spread for sandwiches as an alternative to butter or margarine.
- Dill has been known to have soothing and sedative properties since the time of the Egyptians. Early settlers took dill to America where it became known as 'meeting house seeds' because chewing the seeds helped tummy rumblings during long sermons.

Smoked haddock tartlets

These tartlets make a very pretty starter, perfect for a dinner party. Or serve them as a light lunch dish for 2, with a tomato, basil and cos lettuce salad and chunks of French bread.

Serves 4

Tartlet shells

15 g (½ oz) butter, melted

2 tsp extra virgin olive oil

8 sheets filo pastry, about 125 g (4½ oz) in total

Smoked haddock filling

200 g (7 oz) skinless smoked haddock fillet

200 ml (7 fl oz) semi-skimmed milk

1 bay leaf

10 g (¼ oz) butter

2 large shallots, finely chopped

1 garlic clove, very finely chopped

225 g (8 oz) celeriac, grated

2 tbsp plain flour

1 tsp grated lemon zest

freshly grated nutmeg

2 tsp lemon juice, or to taste

3 tbsp chopped parsley

salt and pepper

fresh flat-leaf parsley to garnish

Preparation and cooking time: about 1 hour

Each serving provides

kcal 278, **protein** 17 g, **fat** 9 g (of which saturated fat 4 g), **carbohydrate** 35 g (of which sugars 4 g), **fibre** 3 g

✓✓✓	B_1, B_6, niacin
✓	A, B_{12}, C, folate, calcium, iron, potassium, selenium

1 To make the tartlet shells, combine the melted butter and olive oil in a small bowl. Lightly brush four 10 cm (4 in) tartlet tins with the mixture. Using a 15 cm (6 in) plate as a guide, cut out 16 rounds of filo pastry. Layer 4 filo rounds in each lightly oiled tin (the pastry will come up above the tops of the tins), brushing each round sparingly with the oil and butter mixture. Chill while making the filling.

2 Put the haddock, milk and bay leaf in a small saucepan, cutting the fish to fit if necessary. Cover and simmer over a low heat for 8–10 minutes or until the fish will flake easily (the milk should hardly boil). Strain the milk and reserve for the sauce. Flake the fish and set aside.

3 Preheat the oven to 190ºC (375ºF, gas mark 5) and put a baking sheet in the oven to heat. Melt the butter in a non-stick saucepan over a moderate heat. Add the shallots and garlic, cover and cook, stirring frequently, for 5 minutes or until the shallots are soft. Add the celeriac and 1 tbsp water, reduce the heat to low and cover again. Continue cooking for 5 minutes.

4 Put the flour in a small bowl and stir in 2 tbsp of cold water to make a thick paste. Gradually add the milk used to poach the fish, stirring to make a smooth liquid. Add to the celeriac and slowly bring to the boil, stirring constantly until thickened. Stir in the lemon zest and a generous grating of nutmeg. Reduce the heat and simmer, stirring frequently, for 8–10 minutes or until the celeriac is tender.

5 Meanwhile, put the tartlet shells on the hot baking sheet and bake for 5 minutes or until the pastry is golden. Carefully remove the pastry shells from the tins and set on the baking sheet. Reduce the oven temperature to 160ºC (325ºF, gas mark 3) and bake for a further 4–5 minutes or until the bases are lightly browned.

6 Gently stir the flaked haddock, lemon juice and parsley into the sauce, and season with salt and pepper to taste. Set the tartlet shells on warm plates and spoon in the fish mixture. Garnish with parsley leaves and serve.

Plus points

- Filo pastry has a much lower fat content than other types of pastry and therefore is a healthier alternative – as long as you are sparing with the oil and butter for brushing.
- Celeriac is the starch-storing lower stem of a special variety of celery. Unlike celery, the swollen stem rather than the stalk is eaten. It provides potassium and vitamin C as well as soluble fibre, the type that helps to lower blood cholesterol levels.

Some more ideas

- For easy entertaining the tartlet shells and filling can be made up to 1 day ahead. Chill the filling, and store the baked tartlet shells in an airtight box. To serve, arrange the tartlet shells on a hot baking sheet, spoon in the filling and reheat in a 180°C (350°F, gas mark 4) oven for about 15 minutes.

- Fill the tartlet shells with a Mediterranean prawn and vegetable mixture. Heat 1½ tbsp extra virgin olive oil in a frying pan over a moderate heat. Add 1 chopped onion, 2 seeded and chopped peppers, and 2 finely chopped garlic cloves. Cook, stirring frequently, for 3–4 minutes or until the onion has softened. Stir in 1 can chopped tomatoes, about 400 g, with the juice, 1 tbsp tomato purée and 2 medium-sized courgettes, sliced. Cover and cook for 8–10 minutes, stirring frequently, until the peppers are just tender. Gently stir in 200 g (7 oz) cooked peeled prawns. Season with salt and pepper to taste and divide among the 4 warm tartlet shells. Garnish with chopped fresh parsley and a few stoned black olives.

Thai fish cakes with dipping sauce

These delicious fish cakes, made with fresh haddock and potatoes, are flavoured with lemongrass and coriander, and spiced with Thai red curry paste. They're served with a tangy lime and honey dipping sauce, and a lettuce, cucumber and mint salad, to make a tempting and nutritious first course.

Serves 8
340 g (12 oz) floury potatoes, peeled and cut into chunks
340 g (12 oz) haddock fillet
juice of 1 lime
1 thin lemongrass stalk, thinly sliced and lightly crushed
2 tsp Thai red curry paste
3 spring onions, thinly sliced
3 garlic cloves, chopped
3 tbsp chopped fresh coriander
1 tsp finely chopped fresh root ginger
4 tbsp plain flour
2 eggs, lightly beaten
100 g (3½ oz) fresh breadcrumbs
2 tbsp extra virgin olive oil
salt

Lime and honey dipping sauce
juice of 3 limes
2 tbsp clear honey
1 tsp chopped fresh root ginger
2 tsp soy sauce
¾ tsp Thai red curry paste
1 fresh mild red chilli, seeded and thinly sliced

Salad
1 round lettuce, finely shredded
½ cucumber, diced
15 g (½ oz) fresh mint leaves, finely shredded

Preparation time: 40 minutes, plus 1 hour chilling
Cooking time: about 12 minutes

1 Place the potatoes in a saucepan and pour over enough boiling water to cover by 5 cm (2 in). Bring back to the boil, then reduce the heat and cook the potatoes for 15–20 minutes or until tender. Drain well, then mash.

2 While the potatoes are cooking, put the haddock in a shallow pan with enough cold water to cover and add half of the lime juice. Bring to the boil, then reduce the heat to low and simmer for 1 minute. Remove from the heat, cover the pan and leave the fish to cool in the liquid for about 4 minutes. Drain the fish and flake the flesh with a fork, discarding the skin and any bones.

3 Mix together the potatoes and fish with a fork, adding the lemongrass, curry paste, spring onions, garlic, coriander, ginger, salt to taste and the remaining lime juice.

4 Tip the flour onto a plate. Pour the eggs onto a second plate. Sprinkle the breadcrumbs on a third plate. Take about 1 tbsp of the fish mixture and shape into a mini fish cake. Turn first in the flour, shaking off the excess, then dip into the egg and, finally, coat with crumbs, turning and pressing on the crumbs to coat all sides evenly. Shape and coat the remaining fish cakes in the same way, making 24 altogether. Chill the fish cakes for 1 hour.

5 Heat half of the oil in a non-stick frying pan. Add half of the fish cakes and cook over a moderate heat for about 3 minutes on each side or until lightly golden and crisp. Remove and keep warm while you cook the rest of the fish cakes, using the remaining oil.

6 Meanwhile, make the dipping sauce. Put all of the ingredients in a small pan and heat gently for 1 minute. Do not boil. Mix together the lettuce, cucumber and mint for the salad. Arrange the fish cakes on individual plates with the salad and serve each with a tiny dish of the dipping sauce.

Plus points
- Recent research suggests that garlic may help to reduce high blood cholesterol levels and inhibit blood clotting, thereby reducing the risk of heart disease and strokes.
- Honey has been used since ancient times as a food, sweetener and preservative. It is sweeter than sugar because of the fructose content and lower in calories, weight for weight, because of its water content.

Some more ideas
- For Middle Eastern salmon cakes with lemon and mint dipping sauce, use fresh salmon fillet instead of the haddock. Replace the lime juice with lemon juice, and instead of lemongrass and Thai curry paste use ½ tsp ground cumin, ½ tsp paprika and a generous shake of Tabasco sauce or cayenne pepper to taste. For the dipping sauce, mix together 3 tbsp mayonnaise (reduced-fat, if you like) and 3 tbsp plain low-fat yogurt until smooth, then stir in ½ tsp paprika, ¼ tsp ground cumin, the juice of 1 lemon and 2 tbsp chopped fresh mint.
- Crab meat – fresh or canned – can be used instead of part or all of the haddock. Canned crab meat should be drained well.

Each serving provides
kcal 295, **protein** 19 g, **fat** 7 g (of which saturated fat 1 g), **carbohydrate** 41 g (of which sugars 8 g), **fibre** 3 g

✓✓✓	B_1, B_6, niacin
✓✓	B_{12}, iron
✓	C, folate, calcium, copper, potassium, selenium

Salmon and watercress pots

This fresh salmon pâté is simple and quick to make. Served with a refreshing watercress salad and crisp Melba toasts or thinly sliced rye bread, it is an excellent starter before a vegetable or grain-based dish.

Serves 4
250 g (8½ oz) piece of salmon fillet
1 bay leaf
2–3 onion slices
5 black peppercorns
200 g (7 oz) smoked salmon slices
200 g (7 oz) fromage frais
3 tbsp crème fraîche
finely grated zest of ½ lemon
1 tbsp lemon juice
1 tsp horseradish sauce
4 tbsp chopped fresh watercress
salt and pepper

Watercress salad
2 tbsp orange juice
1 tbsp sunflower oil
1 tsp Dijon mustard
½ tsp clear honey
100 g (3½ oz) watercress leaves

Preparation time: 25 minutes, plus 1 hour cooling and 2 hours chilling

Each serving provides
kcal 272, **protein** 31 g, **fat** 14 g (of which saturated fat 3 g), **carbohydrate** 6 g (of which sugars 6 g), **fibre** 1 g

✓✓✓	B_1, B_6, B_{12}, niacin
✓✓	A, C, E, selenium
✓	B_2, folate, calcium, iron, potassium, zinc

1. Place the salmon fillet in a shallow pan with the bay leaf, onion slices and peppercorns. Cover with cold water and bring to the boil. Simmer for 1 minute, then remove from the heat and allow the salmon to cool in the liquid for 1 hour.

2. Meanwhile, use the smoked salmon slices to line 4 lightly oiled ramekin dishes, allowing the excess salmon to hang over the sides.

3. Drain the salmon fillet and flake the flesh, discarding the skin and any bones. Put the fish in a food processor or blender with the fromage frais, crème fraîche, lemon zest and juice, horseradish and salt and pepper to taste. Process until smooth. Alternatively, for a coarse-textured pâté, use a fork to mix and mash the flaked fish with the other ingredients.

4. Spoon half of the salmon pâté into the smoked salmon-lined dishes. Mix the chopped watercress into the remaining pâté, then divide among the ramekins. Fold back the overhanging smoked salmon and press down lightly to flatten the tops. Chill for 2 hours.

5. When ready to serve, mix together the orange juice, oil, mustard and honey in a bowl. Add the watercress and toss. Spoon the salad onto 4 plates, then turn out a salmon pot onto each one.

Plus points
- Salmon contains omega-3 polyunsaturated fatty acids, which can help to prevent arteries clogging up and therefore play a part in protecting against strokes and heart attacks.
- Watercress provides good amounts of several antioxidants, including vitamin C, vitamin E and beta-carotene. Like all dark green vegetables, watercress also contains substantial amounts of folate.

Some more ideas
- Make the pâté with canned salmon, which will be higher in calcium due to the bones it contains. Drain a can of red salmon, about 212 g, and remove any skin. Mash the fish with 200 g (7 oz) reduced-fat soft cheese with chives, 3 tbsp mayonnaise and ½ tsp Tabasco sauce. Season with plenty of freshly ground black pepper. Spoon half of the pâté into the smoked salmon-lined ramekin dishes, top each with 1 tbsp chopped watercress and spoon over the remaining pâté. Make the salad with mixed rocket and spinach leaves.
- Omit the smoked salmon slices. Double the quantity of watercress and mix into all of the pâté at the end of step 3, then serve as a delicious dip with a selection of vegetable strips and bread sticks or warm pitta bread fingers.

Sesame prawn and crab toasts

Inspired by the small crispy prawn toasts served in Chinese restaurants, these can be served as a starter or they make a good savoury nibble to hand round with drinks. Traditionally the toasts are deep fried in oil, but in this updated healthy version they are baked in a hot oven until crisp and golden.

Serves 4

Prawn and crab topping

85 g (3 oz) peeled raw prawns, very finely chopped
85 g (3 oz) fresh white crab meat, flaked
2 spring onions, thinly sliced
1 large garlic clove, crushed
½ small red pepper, seeded and diced
½ tsp finely grated lemon zest
pinch of cayenne pepper
1 tbsp double cream

Toasts

2 tbsp double cream
1 large egg
2 large slices of oatmeal or soft grain bread
2 tsp sesame seeds
salt and pepper
shredded spring onions to garnish

Preparation time: 15 minutes
Cooking time: 20–25 minutes

1 Preheat the oven to 200°C (400°F, gas mark 6). Put the prawns, crab meat, spring onions, garlic, red pepper, lemon zest, cayenne pepper and cream into a bowl and mix well to make a spreadable paste. Season with salt and pepper to taste and set aside until ready to cook. (If you want to prepare the mixture ahead, it can be kept in the fridge for 4 hours.)

2 Beat together the cream and egg until smooth. Dip the bread in the mixture to coat both sides, then place on a greased baking sheet. Spread the fish mixture evenly over the bread, right up to the edges.

3 Lightly brush the remaining egg and cream mixture over the surface of the fish mixture and sprinkle evenly with the sesame seeds.

4 Bake for 20–25 minutes or until crisp and golden. Cut each slice of toast into 8 triangles and serve immediately, garnished with shredded spring onions.

Another idea

- For five-spice prawn and water chestnut toasts, omit the crab meat and use 170 g (6 oz) prawns. Season with a generous pinch of five-spice powder instead of the cayenne pepper and lemon zest. Instead of the red pepper, stir in 6 water chestnuts, very finely chopped, and 4 tsp chopped fresh coriander.

Each serving provides

kcal 197, **protein** 13 g, **fat** 12 g (of which saturated fat 5 g), **carbohydrate** 10 g (of which sugars 2 g), **fibre** 1 g

✓✓✓	B_1, B_6, B_{12}, niacin
✓✓	A, C, copper
✓	B_2, E, iron, selenium, zinc

Plus points

- Crab is a good source of phosphorus which is not only essential for healthy bones and teeth but is also needed for the release of energy from food.
- Sesame seeds can be an important source of protein, particularly for vegetarians. The oil extracted from sesame seeds is high in polyunsaturated fatty acids, which can help to prevent heart disease.
- Healthy eating recommendations are to increase the intake of complex or starchy carbohydrates. This can easily be achieved by eating more bread, particularly as there is now such a variety to choose from.

Grilled oysters with fennel and spinach topping

For some people, just slipping oysters down raw is the only way to eat them, but if you prefer them cooked, this is a great way to prepare them. Topped with a mixture of potato, fennel and spinach, they make a substantial starter. Ask the fishmonger to open the oysters for you. Serve with warm pitta bread slices.

Serves 4
16 oysters in the shell, opened and top shell discarded
30 g (1 oz) butter
1 shallot, finely chopped
100 g (3½ oz) potato, peeled and finely diced
100 g (3½ oz) bulb of fennel, finely diced
100 g (3½ oz) spinach, torn into pieces
1 tbsp lemon juice
2 tbsp chopped parsley
salt and pepper
lemon wedges to serve

Preparation time: 25 minutes
Cooking time: about 3 minutes

1 Check the oysters to make sure there are no bits of shattered shell on them. Arrange them, on their half shells, in four individual flameproof dishes, or on one large dish, and season with salt and pepper to taste. (Propping the shells with crumpled foil will prevent them from tipping.)

2 Preheat the grill to moderate. Heat the butter in a frying pan, add the shallot and cook over a gentle heat for 2 minutes or until beginning to soften. Add the diced potato and fennel and cook gently for 10 minutes or until tender, stirring occasionally.

3 Stir in the spinach and cook for 1–2 minutes or until the spinach has just wilted. Add the lemon juice, parsley and seasoning to taste. Spoon 1 tbsp of the mixture over each oyster.

4 Cook the oysters under the grill for 3 minutes or until the topping is tinged brown. Serve immediately, with lemon wedges.

Some more ideas
• For a spicy almond topping, use 55 g (2 oz) slivered almonds instead of potatoes. Roughly chop the nuts in a blender or food processor, or by hand, and mix with 1–2 garlic cloves, finely chopped, 2 tbsp chopped fresh coriander, ½ small red chilli, seeded and finely chopped, 1 tsp ground cumin, 1 tsp paprika and 1 tbsp extra virgin olive oil. Add this mixture to the cooked shallot and fennel, together with 55 g (2 oz) white breadcrumbs and the juice of ½ lemon. Mix well, then add the spinach and finish as in the main recipe.

• Replace the fennel and spinach with 55 g (2 oz) smoked back bacon, finely chopped, and 100 g (3½ oz) Savoy cabbage, finely shredded. Add some toasted cumin seeds or caraway seeds for extra flavour.

Each serving provides
kcal 101, protein 4 g, fat 7 g (of which saturated fat 4 g), carbohydrate 6 g (of which sugars 1 g), fibre 2 g

✓✓✓	B_1, B_6, B_{12}, niacin, copper, zinc
✓✓	A, iron
✓	C, folate, calcium, potassium

Plus points
• Oysters have long been linked with aphrodisiac powers, probably because they are an excellent source of zinc which is essential for growth and sexual maturity.
• Although spinach appears to be an excellent source of iron, the iron isn't easily absorbed by the body. However, the vitamin C from the lemon juice in this recipe will help the absorption.

For Maximum Vitality

Healthy fish salads packed with good things

THE WIDE VARIETY OF FISH AND SHELLFISH combines well with crunchy raw vegetables and sweet, juicy fruits to make wonderful salads. With starchy carbohydrate from the addition of bulghur wheat, rice, pasta or potatoes, these salads can make well-balanced meals. For a taste of summer, try a mix of prawns, melon and mango, or crab and avocado. In cooler weather, enjoy a smoked trout, pasta and pepper salad, or a warm fish salad, such as grilled spiced salmon with papaya and orange, or a trio of poached seafood with spinach, carrot and courgette.

Crab and avocado salad

Fresh crab is a real summertime treat. It is rich in flavour and combines well in a salad with crunchy apples and bean sprouts, chunks of perfectly ripe avocados and nutty-flavoured bulghur wheat.

Serves 4

Bulghur wheat salad
200 g (7 oz) bulghur wheat
1 tbsp extra virgin olive oil
3 tbsp lemon juice
3 tbsp chopped fresh flat-leaf parsley
1 tbsp snipped fresh chives
2 medium-sized tomatoes, diced
salt and pepper

Crab salad
340 g (12 oz) fresh white crab meat
2 avocados
2 crisp green dessert apples
125 g (4½ oz) bean sprouts
3 tbsp mayonnaise
3 tbsp plain low-fat yogurt
1 tbsp lemon juice
small pinch of cayenne pepper
2 Little Gem lettuces, separated into leaves
55 g (2 oz) walnut halves, toasted and roughly chopped

Preparation time: 40 minutes, plus cooling

Each serving provides
kcal 641, **protein** 28 g, **fat** 36 g (of which saturated fat 5 g), **carbohydrate** 53 g (of which sugars 12.5 g), **fibre** 5 g

✓✓✓	B_1, B_6, niacin, copper
✓✓	B_2, C, E iron, potassium, zinc
✓	A, folate, calcium, selenium

1. Put the bulghur wheat in a large saucepan with 1.3 litres (2¼ pints) cold water. Bring to the boil over a high heat, then reduce the heat and simmer for 10–15 minutes or until the grains are just tender. Drain in a large sieve, pressing down well to squeeze out all the excess water. Leave to cool.

2. Combine the oil, lemon juice, parsley, chives and diced tomatoes in a large mixing bowl. Add the bulghur wheat and mix thoroughly, then season with salt and pepper to taste. Leave to stand at room temperature while preparing the crab salad.

3. Pick over and flake the crab meat, discarding any fragments of shell. Halve, stone and peel the avocados, then chop the flesh. Add to the crab. Quarter and core the apples, then thinly slice them. Add to the crab meat with the bean sprouts.

4. Mix the mayonnaise with the yogurt until smooth. Add the lemon juice and cayenne pepper. Spoon onto the crab mixture and toss very gently until just combined.

5. Pile the bulghur salad onto a serving platter and arrange the Little Gem leaves on top. Spoon the crab salad onto the leaves and scatter over the walnuts. Serve immediately.

Plus points
- Although yogurt has been used for its nutritional and medicinal properties for hundreds of years in the Middle and Far East and Eastern Europe, it has only become popular in this country in the past few decades. Like other dairy products yogurt is a good source of calcium. This mineral is recognised mainly for its involvement with maintaining healthy bones, but it is also vital for the proper functioning of muscles and nerves and for blood clotting.
- Walnuts have a high fat content, but this is mostly in the form of polyunsaturated fat rather than saturated fat. Walnuts are a good source of the antioxidant nutrients selenium, zinc, copper and vitamin E.

Some more ideas
- Canned crab meat makes an excellent salad base. Use 2 cans, about 170 g each, well drained, instead of the fresh crab.
- Use 200 g (7 oz) basmati rice instead of the bulghur wheat. Cook the rice in boiling water for 10–12 minutes, or according to the packet instructions, until tender. Drain, rinse with cold water and drain again, then leave to dry before mixing with the dressing and tomatoes.

Trio of warm seafood salad

Many different fish work well in this salad, so you can see what is the freshest at the fishmonger and make up your own mixture. Choose firm-fleshed white or oily fish and some shellfish. Serve with crusty bread.

Serves 4

Salad
100 g (3½ oz) baby spinach leaves
1 Little Gem lettuce
1 small carrot
1 small courgette

Fish mixture
600 g (1 lb 5 oz) mussels, scrubbed and beards removed
300 ml (10 fl oz) fish stock, preferably home-made (see page 27)
1 shallot, finely chopped
1 carrot, finely diced
1 celery stick, thinly sliced
2 thick parsley stalks
300 g (10½ oz) skinless halibut fillet
8 queen scallops, about 100 g (3½ oz) in total
2 tbsp extra virgin olive oil
grated zest and juice of ½ lemon
salt and pepper

To garnish
2 tbsp chopped fresh flat-leaf parsley
sprigs of fresh dill

Preparation and cooking time: 40 minutes

Each serving provides
kcal 227, protein 30 g, fat 9 g (of which saturated fat 1 g), carbohydrate 6.5 g (of which sugars 4 g), fibre 2 g

✓✓✓	A, B_1, B_6, B_{12}, niacin, iron
✓✓	C, folate, selenium
✓	E, calcium, copper, potassium, zinc

1 Divide the spinach leaves among 4 plates. Tear or shred the Little Gem lettuce and sprinkle over the spinach. With a vegetable peeler, make short curly ribbon shavings of carrot and courgette, and arrange them in the centre of the spinach and lettuce.

2 Put the mussels in a large saucepan and add 2 tbsp of the stock. Cover tightly and cook over a high heat for 2–3 minutes, shaking the pan occasionally, until the shells have opened.

3 Tip the mussels into a colander over a large bowl, shaking them to make sure you catch all the cooking juices. Remove the mussels from the shells, discarding any mussels that have not opened. Set the mussels aside.

4 Pour the remaining stock and the reserved cooking juices into the saucepan. Add the shallot, carrot, celery and parsley stalks. Cover and bring to the boil, then simmer for 5 minutes. Remove the parsley stalks.

5 Cut the halibut into 2.5 cm (1 in) chunks. Add the halibut and scallops to the cooking liquid, cover again and poach gently for 2 minutes. Add the mussels and poach for a further 1 minute or until all the fish is just cooked. Remove the fish from the liquid with a large draining spoon and put it onto a warm plate. Boil the liquid until it has reduced by half – about 200 ml (7 fl oz). Meanwhile, divide the seafood and cooked vegetables among the prepared plates, piling them in the middle of the salad.

6 Whisk the oil and lemon zest and juice into the reduced cooking liquid, and season with salt and pepper to taste. Spoon this hot dressing over the fish, vegetables and salad, and sprinkle with the chopped parsley and dill. Serve immediately.

Plus points

- Although classified as a white fish, most of which are low in fat, halibut does contain some fat – about the same amount as in skinless chicken breast. The fat is present predominantly as polyunsaturated and monounsaturated fatty acids, which can help to improve health.
- Although carrots are recognised as a good source of vitamin A from the beta-carotene they contain, the amount provided depends on the variety and age of the carrot. Older and darker orange carrots contain more beta-carotene than young, pale orange ones.
- Spinach is a good source of many antioxidant nutrients, including vitamins C and E. It also contains substantial amounts of many of the B vitamins, including folate, niacin and B_6.

Some more ideas

• Instead of mussels, halibut and scallops, make the salad with salmon, cod or pollack and prawns. Use 225 g (8 oz) skinless salmon fillet, 170 g (6 oz) skinless cod or pollack fillet and 12 raw tiger prawns, peeled. Cut the salmon and cod into 2.5 cm (1 in) pieces. Add the thicker pieces of fish to the stock with the prawns and poach for 2 minutes, then add the thinner pieces of salmon and cod and poach for a further 1–1½ minutes. Serve the seafood on a salad made from 100 g (3½ oz) mixed lamb's lettuce and baby Oak Leaf lettuce, 1 Little Gem lettuce, shredded or torn into pieces, 100 g (3½ oz) celeriac, grated, and 1 pear, quartered, cored and sliced.

• Other fish to try with mussels, scallops or prawns include monkfish, swordfish and tuna.

• Add a few blanched fine green beans, asparagus spears or samphire to the salad.

• Make the salad with watercress, orange segments and thinly sliced bulb fennel.

• You can vary the herbs in this recipe – fennel, basil, chervil and chives all go well with the fish.

for maximum vitality

Lobster salad with lime dressing

A ready-cooked lobster makes a luxurious salad for 2 people to share. The firm, sweet flavoured lobster meat is here served on a bed of peppery salad leaves, shredded mange-tout, grapes and tiny new potatoes cooked in their skins, all tossed with a dressing spiked with lime zest. Serve with country-style bread.

Serves 2

250 g (8½ oz) baby red-skinned new potatoes, scrubbed
2 tbsp mayonnaise
2 tbsp Greek-style yogurt
finely grated zest of ½ lime
1 cooked lobster, about 500 g (1 lb 2 oz)
2 small shallots, thinly sliced
85 g (3 oz) mange-tout, shredded
85 g (3 oz) seedless red grapes
85 g (3 oz) seedless green grapes
30 g (1 oz) watercress
55 g (2 oz) rocket leaves
salt and pepper

Preparation time: 1 hour

1 Put the potatoes in a saucepan and cover with boiling water. Cook for about 15 minutes or until just tender. Drain and leave to cool, then cut the potatoes in half.

2 While the potatoes are cooling, mix together the mayonnaise, yogurt and lime zest, and season with salt and pepper to taste. Set aside.

3 Pull and twist off the lobster claws and set aside. With a sharp knife, cut the body in half lengthways, from tail end through the head. Remove the meat from the body/tail shell and the claws. Chop all the meat into chunks. (The meat from the spindly legs can also be removed with tweezers, but this takes a lot of effort for the small amount of meat inside them.)

4 Toss the potatoes with the shallots, mange-tout, grapes, watercress and lime dressing. Arrange the rocket on large plates and add the watercress and potato salad. Scatter the lobster meat on top and serve.

Some more ideas

- For a lightly curried lime and honey dressing, mix 2 tbsp groundnut oil with 1 tbsp lemon juice, ½ tsp curry paste and ½ tsp clear honey.
- To make a lobster and papaya salad, instead of the mange-tout and grapes, toss 1 large ripe papaya, seeded and sliced, and 1 chopped avocado with the potatoes, watercress and shallots. Pile the papaya salad onto 85 g (3 oz) herb salad leaves (containing sprigs of fresh coriander) rather than rocket. Drizzle with the curried lime and honey dressing above and scatter over the lobster meat and 30 g (1 oz) toasted cashew nuts.
- Chicory or shredded romaine or cos lettuce can be used instead of the rocket.

Each serving provides

kcal 407, **protein** 27 g, **fat** 17 g (of which saturated fat 4 g), **carbohydrate** 39 g (of which sugars 20 g), **fibre** 4 g

✓✓✓	B_1, B_6, B_{12}, C, niacin, copper, selenium
✓✓	A, E, calcium, iron, potassium, zinc
✓	B_2, folate

Plus points

- Lobster is an excellent source of the antioxidant selenium, which helps to protect cells from damage by free radicals.
- Some varieties of grape are cultivated for wine, others for drying to become raisins, currants and sultanas, and others for just eating. The nutrient content of different coloured grapes is very similar. Of all fruits, grapes have one of the highest sugar contents – mainly as glucose and fructose – and they are a good source of potassium.

for maximum vitality

Marinated kipper salad

This old-fashioned way of cooking kippers in a jug of boiling water keeps the flesh moist and tender and it also eliminates the strong smells associated with grilling kippers. Serve the kipper salad with Granary bread.

Serves 4
4 kippers, about 170 g (6 oz) each
2½ tbsp extra virgin olive oil
2 tbsp cider vinegar
1 small onion, finely chopped
1 bay leaf
200 g (7 oz) baby spinach leaves
150 g (5½ oz) cucumber, diced
1 large carrot, grated
3 spring onions, thinly sliced
1 crisp red dessert apple
2 tbsp chopped parsley
1 tbsp chopped fresh chervil
1 tbsp chopped fresh dill
salt and pepper

Preparation time: 30 minutes, plus 24 hours marinating

Each serving provides
kcal 498, protein 32 g, fat 37 g (of which saturated fat 6 g), carbohydrate 9 g (of which sugars 8 g), fibre 3 g

✓✓✓	A, B_6, B_{12}, niacin, iron, selenium
✓✓	B_1, C, folate, calcium, potassium
✓	B_2, E, copper, zinc

1. To cook the kippers, remove the heads and place the fish in a heatproof jug, tails upwards. Pour in boiling water, making sure the kippers are covered up to their tails. Leave for 5–8 minutes or until the flesh will flake easily. Use tongs to remove the kippers from the liquid and pat them dry on kitchen paper. Leave to cool.

2. Meanwhile, make the marinade. Mix together 2 tbsp of the oil, the vinegar, onion and bay leaf in a non-metallic dish.

3. As soon as the kippers are cool enough to handle, flake the flesh into pieces, discarding the skin and bones. Add the fish to the marinade and toss gently. Set aside until cool, then cover and chill for up to 24 hours.

4. To prepare the salad, put the spinach leaves in a bowl and add the cucumber, carrot and spring onions. Core and dice the apple and add to the bowl. Toss all the ingredients together gently.

5. Discard the bay leaf from the kippers. Add the kippers and any remaining marinade to the salad ingredients and toss gently. Add the parsley, chervil and dill and toss again. Season with salt and pepper to taste and sprinkle over the remaining ½ tbsp oil. Serve at once.

Some more ideas
- To make this into a more substantial salad, and boost the starchy carbohydrates, add some potatoes. Cook 500 g (1 lb 2 oz) scrubbed new potatoes in boiling water until tender. Drain and leave until cool enough to handle, then cut into bite-sized pieces. Add ½ tbsp wholegrain mustard to the marinade, and add the potatoes to the marinade with the kippers.
- Watercress or rocket leaves can be used instead of the spinach, or a mixture of leaves.

Plus points
- Kippers are herrings that have been split, lightly salted and then cold-smoked. They are a good source of vitamin B_{12}, which is needed for the formation of red blood cells and to maintain a healthy nervous system.
- Apples contain good amounts of vitamin C and soluble fibre. Research has shown that eating apples has benefits for teeth too, as it can help to prevent gum disease.
- Chervil is a herb used since Roman times, particularly popular in French cuisine where it is used to flavour soups and sauces. As with many herbs, it is believed to help stimulate the digestive process.

Provençal tuna and pepper salad

This colourful salad is full of varied flavours and textures. Chunks of tuna, wedges of potato, crisp beans and tangy tomatoes – one bite is like a visit to Provence. Serve with crusty baguettes.

Serves 4

400 g (14 oz) new potatoes
55 g (2 oz) fine green beans
6 quail's eggs
225 g (8 oz) mixed salad leaves
1 tbsp chopped parsley
1 tbsp snipped fresh chives
1 small red onion, thinly sliced
1 tbsp tapenade (black olive paste)
2 garlic cloves, chopped
2 tbsp extra virgin olive oil
1 tbsp red wine vinegar
1 tsp balsamic vinegar
10–15 radishes, thinly sliced
1 can tuna in spring water, about 200 g, drained
100 g (3½ oz) cherry tomatoes
1 red pepper, seeded and thinly sliced
1 yellow pepper, seeded and thinly sliced
1 green pepper, seeded and thinly sliced
8 black olives
salt and pepper
fresh basil leaves to garnish

Preparation time: 45 minutes

Each serving provides
kcal 296, **protein** 20 g, **fat** 13 g (of which saturated fat 2 g), **carbohydrate** 26 g (of which sugars 10 g), **fibre** 5 g

✓✓✓	B_1, B_6, B_{12}, C, niacin, selenium
✓✓	A, folate, iron, potassium
✓	B_2, E, calcium, copper, zinc

1. Place the potatoes in a saucepan and cover with boiling water. Cook over a moderate heat for 10 minutes. Add the beans and cook for a further 5 minutes or until the potatoes are tender and the beans are just cooked. Drain well and set aside to cool.

2. Put the quail's eggs into a saucepan with cold water to cover and bring to the boil. Reduce the heat and cook at a low simmer for 3 minutes. Rinse well in cold water. Peel the eggs carefully and place in cold water.

3. Toss the salad leaves with the parsley, chives and red onion in a large shallow bowl.

4. To make the dressing, mix the tapenade with the garlic, olive oil, red wine vinegar and balsamic vinegar, and season with salt and pepper to taste. Pour two-thirds of the dressing over the salad leaves and toss well to mix.

5. Halve the potatoes and arrange them on top of the leaves with the green beans, radishes, chunks of tuna, tomatoes, peppers and olives. Halve the quail's eggs and add them to the salad. Pour over the remaining dressing, garnish with basil leaves and serve.

Some more ideas

- For a classic Italian cannellini bean and tuna salad, omit the potatoes and quail's eggs and add 1 can cannellini beans, about 400 g, well drained, to the salad leaves. Use the juice of ½ lemon in the dressing instead of balsamic vinegar.

- Try this salad using different varieties of tomatoes, such as yellow cherry tomatoes, baby plum tomatoes or quartered vine-ripened plum tomatoes.

Plus points

- Canned tuna retains a high vitamin content, particularly vitamins B_{12} and D.
- In common with many other salad ingredients, radishes are a useful source of vitamin C and are very low in calories. The radish has a very hot flavour due to an enzyme in the skin that reacts with another substance to form a mustard type of oil.
- Green beans are a good source of dietary fibre and provide valuable amounts of folate.

Smoked trout and pasta salad

Tempt your family with this delicious heart-healthy pasta salad. It makes an ideal midweek supper served with ciabatta bread. If you wait until the last minute to add the rocket leaves, it won't spoil if anyone's late home.

Serves 4

- 1 red pepper, seeded and quartered
- 1 yellow pepper, seeded and quartered
- 280 g (10 oz) penne rigati (ridged penne) or other pasta shapes
- 2 smoked trout fillets, about 140 g (5 oz) each
- 1 orange
- 1 large avocado
- 2 spring onions, sliced
- 2 tbsp bottled capers, well drained
- 50 g (1¾ oz) rocket leaves

Dill and lemon dressing

- 4 tbsp fromage frais
- 2 tsp lemon juice
- 1 tsp Dijon mustard
- 2 tbsp chopped fresh dill
- ½ tsp caster sugar
- salt and pepper

Preparation time: 40 minutes

1. Preheat the grill to high. Place the peppers on the grill rack, skin side up, and grill for about 10 minutes or until the skins are blistered and blackened. Remove from the grill and place in a polythene bag. Seal and set aside to cool.

2. Meanwhile, bring a large pan of water to the boil and add the pasta shapes. Cook for 10–12 minutes, or according to the packet instructions, until al dente. Drain, rinse under cold running water and drain well again. Tip the pasta into a large salad bowl.

3. Flake the trout fillets into bite-sized pieces, discarding the skin and any bones. Cut all the skin and pith from the orange and cut out the segments from between the membranes. Halve the segments. Halve, stone and peel the avocado, and cut into small chunks. Mix together the dressing ingredients and season with salt and pepper to taste.

4. Peel the peppers and cut them into strips. Add the peppers to the pasta together with the trout, orange, avocado, spring onions and capers. Add the dressing and toss gently but thoroughly. Just before serving, toss the rocket leaves into the salad.

Some more ideas

- For a prawn and pasta salad, add 200 g (7 oz) peeled cooked prawns instead of the trout, and replace the peppers and orange with 200 g (7 oz) peeled, chopped pineapple.
- Make a lime and basil dressing by using 1 tbsp lime juice instead of the lemon juice, and chopped fresh basil instead of the dill.
- Toss 100 g (3½ oz) baby spinach leaves into the pasta salad instead of the rocket.

Each serving provides

kcal 525, **protein** 28 g, **fat** 18 g (of which saturated fat 5 g), **carbohydrate** 66.5 g (of which sugars 14 g), **fibre** 6 g

✓✓✓	A, B_1, B_6, B_{12}, C, niacin
✓✓	E, copper, potassium, selenium
✓	B_2, folate, calcium, iron, zinc

Plus points

- Smoked trout is usually prepared from rainbow trout, and like its fresh counterpart is an excellent source of many vitamins and minerals and of healthy fats.
- Peppers are an excellent source of vitamin C, but the beta-carotene content varies depending on the colour of the pepper. Green peppers contain 265 mcg carotene per 100 g (3½ oz), while red peppers contain 3840 mcg for the same weight.
- There are thought to be over 500 different varieties of pasta eaten in Italy, of which only about 50 are well-known outside Italy. Low in fat and a good source of starchy (complex) carbohydrate, pasta has become one of the world's most popular foods.

Grilled salmon salad

Conjure up the colours and flavours of a tropical island with this unusual warm salad. The rich flavour of salmon is perfectly balanced by the gentle acidity of orange and the sweetness of mango and papaya. Serve with an accompanying salad of mixed long-grain and wild rice or crusty French bread.

Serves 4

8 cardamom pods, crushed
1 tsp cumin seeds
finely grated zest and juice of 1 lime
juice of 1 large orange
1 tbsp light soy sauce
1 tbsp clear honey
4 pieces of skinless salmon fillet, about 115 g (4 oz) each
150 g (5½ oz) mixed colourful salad leaves, such as Lollo Rosso, Oak Leaf lettuce and baby red chard
1 mango, peeled and cut into 1 cm (½ in) cubes
1 papaya, peeled, seeded and cut into 1 cm (½ in) cubes
1 orange, peeled and segmented
salt and pepper

Preparation and cooking time: 30 minutes, plus 30 minutes marinating

Each serving provides
kcal 330, **protein** 25 g, **fat** 13 g (of which saturated fat 2 g), **carbohydrate** 29 g (of which sugars 29 g), **fibre** 5 g

✓✓✓	A, B_1, B_6, B_{12}, C, niacin
✓✓	E, potassium, selenium
✓	folate, calcium, copper, iron, zinc

1 Heat a small frying pan. Scrape the seeds from the cardamom pods, and add them to the hot pan with the cumin seeds. Toast for a few seconds to release the aromas, then tip the cardamom and cumin seeds into a shallow non-metallic dish.

2 Add the lime zest and juice, orange juice, soy sauce and honey to the seeds, and season with salt and pepper to taste. Lay the pieces of salmon fillet in the dish. Turn them over to coat both sides. Cover and leave to marinate for about 30 minutes.

3 Preheat the grill to high. Lift the salmon out of the marinade, place on the grill rack and grill for 4–5 minutes on one side only; the salmon fillets should still be slightly translucent in the centre. Meanwhile, pour the marinade into a small saucepan and bring just to the boil.

4 Arrange the salad leaves in the middle of 4 plates. Scatter the mango and papaya cubes and orange segments over and around the salad. Place the cooked salmon on top of the salad and spoon over the warm marinade. Serve immediately.

Plus points
• Salmon is a useful source of potassium, which is needed for the regulation of fluid balance in the body, to help prevent high blood pressure.
• Papaya is a useful source of vitamin A, in the form of beta-carotene, which helps to maintain good vision. The papaya has a vital role to play in preventing blindness in many parts of the world where few other foods with a vitamin A content are eaten regularly.

Some more ideas
• For an Oriental-style halibut salad, use 4 pieces of skinless halibut fillet, about 140 g (5 oz) each, instead of the salmon. Make a marinade with 2 garlic cloves, crushed, 1 tsp grated fresh root ginger, 1 tsp ground cumin, 1 tsp ground coriander, 2 tbsp rice wine or dry sherry, 1 tbsp fish sauce, the grated zest of 1 lime, the juice of 2 limes and salt to taste. Marinate the halibut for at least 30 minutes, then grill for 5–6 minutes. Strain the marinade and bring just to the boil. Serve the fish on a crunchy salad of bean sprouts, shredded Chinese cabbage, carrot, red pepper and thinly sliced mushrooms, with the warm marinade spooned over.
• Serve the salmon on a bed of stir-fried or steamed courgettes and carrots.

for maximum vitality

Fennel, apple and herring salad

Oily fish such as herring are traditionally served with tart or pungent ingredients that offer a refreshing piquancy to balance the rich fish flavour. In this Scandinavian-style salad, apple, fennel and lemon juice offer the complementary contrast. Serve the salad for lunch or supper.

Serves 4

4 herrings, cleaned and heads removed, cleaned weight about 500 g (1 lb 2 oz) in total
120 ml (4 fl oz) dry cider
360 ml (12 fl oz) vegetable stock
2 shallots, sliced
1 bay leaf
200 g (7 oz) couscous
2 tbsp chopped fresh mint
3 tbsp chopped parsley
1 tbsp lemon juice
1 red-skinned dessert apple
½ cucumber, diced
1 small bulb of fennel, diced
3 spring onions, finely chopped
45 g (1½ oz) hazelnuts, toasted and chopped
salt and pepper
sprigs of fresh dill or fennel fronds to garnish

Dill and mustard dressing

1 tbsp lemon juice
1 tbsp Dijon mustard
2 tbsp mayonnaise
4 tbsp Greek-style yogurt
2 tbsp chopped fresh dill

Preparation time: 45 minutes

1. Rinse the herrings. Pour the cider and stock into a saucepan large enough to hold the fish. Add the shallots and bay leaf, cover and simmer over a moderately low heat for 10 minutes. Add the fish and continue simmering for 8 minutes or until the flesh looks opaque. Remove the herrings and set aside to cool. Strain the cooking liquid and reserve 270 ml (9 fl oz).

2. Put the couscous in a bowl and pour over the reserved fish cooking liquid. Cover and leave to soak for about 10 minutes or until the couscous has absorbed all the liquid. Add the mint, parsley and lemon juice, and fluff up the grains with a fork to mix.

3. To make the dressing, in a small bowl stir together the lemon juice, mustard, mayonnaise and yogurt until smooth, then stir in the dill.

4. Quarter, core and dice the apple. Put the apple, cucumber, fennel, spring onions and hazelnuts into a bowl and stir in half of the dressing. Season with salt and pepper to taste.

5. Remove the skin from the herrings and carefully take the fillets off the backbone. Use tweezers, if necessary, to remove any remaining bones. Cut the flesh into large pieces and mix gently with the remaining dressing.

6. Pile the couscous on individual plates and arrange the apple salad and fish on top. Garnish with dill sprigs or fennel fronds and serve.

Plus points

- Greek-style yogurt is made from full fat cow's or ewe's milk, and it has a much thicker texture and richer taste than plain low-fat yogurt. Look out for the lower fat varieties of Greek-style yogurt now available, with 4% or even 0% fat content – they still retain the creamy texture.
- The fat content of herring (and of the fat-soluble vitamins A and D) varies according to the season, with highest values occurring in late summer and lowest values in spring. Vitamin A is essential for healthy skin, vision and eyes and, as with all vitamins, for growth; vitamin D is vital for the efficient absorption of calcium.

Each serving provides

kcal 562, **protein** 30 g, **fat** 34 g (of which saturated fat 8 g), **carbohydrate** 34 g (of which sugars 8 g), **fibre** 3 g

✓✓✓	B_6, B_{12}, E, niacin, iron, selenium
✓✓	B_1, calcium, copper, potassium
✓	A, B_2, C, folate, zinc

Some more ideas

- Replace the couscous with 280 g (10 oz) small pasta shapes, cooked and cooled. Gently stir the pasta with the herring and the apple salad, adding a little extra dill.
- Make a delicious Italian-style mackerel and bean salad. Wrap a 450 g (1 lb) mackerel in foil and bake in a preheated 180ºC (350ºF, gas mark 4) oven for about 20 minutes. Cool, then remove the skin and bones and flake the flesh. Omit the couscous and the apple salad. Instead, mix together 2 oranges, peeled and segmented, 1 small bulb of fennel, thinly sliced, 3 spring onions, thinly sliced and a can of cannellini or kidney beans, about 400 g, rinsed and drained. Add the mackerel to the salad with 3 tbsp chopped parsley. Make a dressing with 1 tbsp lemon juice, 1 tsp Dijon mustard, 2 tbsp extra virgin olive oil and pepper to taste. Toss the salad with the dressing and serve on a bed of rocket, with crusty bread to accompany.

Prawn, melon and mango salad

A very pretty salad, this combines tiger prawns with colourful, juicy fruits tossed in a light dressing flavoured with honey and fresh mint. It makes a lovely light summer meal, served with bread or rolls.

Serves 4
400 g (14 oz) cooked peeled tiger prawns
1 mango, about 600 g (1 lb 5 oz)
¼ honeydew or ½ Charentais melon, about 340 g (12 oz), cubed
8 cherry tomatoes, halved
100 g (3½ oz) rocket leaves
¼ cucumber, sliced
salt and pepper
fresh mint leaves to garnish

Mint and honey dressing
2 tbsp extra virgin olive oil
juice of 1 lemon
1 tbsp clear honey
2 tbsp chopped fresh mint

Preparation time: 20 minutes, plus at least 30 minutes marinating

1. Whisk together all the ingredients for the dressing in a large bowl and season with salt and pepper to taste. Add the prawns to the dressing, cover and leave to marinate in the fridge for 30 minutes to 1 hour.

2. Halve the mango lengthways, cutting down round each side of the stone. Cut the flesh on each half in a criss-cross fashion to make cubes, then cut the cubes away from the skin.

3. Remove the prawns from the fridge. Add the mango, melon and tomatoes and gently stir together. Arrange the rocket leaves and cucumber slices around the edge of a shallow serving dish, and spoon the prawn salad into the centre. Garnish with sprigs of mint and serve.

Some more ideas
- Use mixed seafood instead of the prawns. Another idea is crabsticks, cut in half.
- To add a slightly spicy note to the salad, mix 15 g (½ oz) fresh root ginger, cut into very fine strips, into the dressing.
- Other fruits can be used in place of the melon and mango. Good combinations include chopped nectarine and halved, seedless white grapes or sliced kiwi fruit with cubes of fresh pineapple.
- To vary the dressing, use the juice of ½ orange in place of the lemon juice and 2 tbsp chopped fresh coriander instead of mint.
- For an attractive presentation, serve the salad in halved Charentais melon shells.

Each serving provides
kcal 253, protein 24 g, fat 7 g (of which saturated fat 1 g), carbohydrate 25 g (of which sugars 24 g), fibre 4 g

✓✓✓	B_1, B_{12}, C, niacin
✓✓	A, copper, iron, selenium, zinc
✓	E, potassium

Plus points
- Fresh mangoes are an excellent source of the important antioxidant beta-carotene, which the body can convert to vitamin A. The amount of beta-carotene on offer varies according to the ripeness of the fruit – levels can range from 300 to 3000 mcg per 100 g (3½ oz) raw mango flesh.
- Melons have an exceptionally high water content, averaging at least 90%, which makes them very refreshing. The varieties with orange flesh, like Charentais, contain beta-carotene.

Fast Fish

Simple suppers in 30 minutes or less

CREATING FAST NUTRITIOUS MEALS is easy with fish and shellfish, as their delicate texture positively benefits from quick cooking. Pan-frying is just one simple and speedy cooking method – try swordfish with a Mexican salad or halibut steaks served with a vibrant salsa. Stir-frying is an excellent way to cook seafood, and scallops and prawns stir-fried with lemon, honey and soy sauce are delicious. Steaming retains all the natural flavours and juices of the fish and takes only minutes, so Chinese-style plaice rolls with samphire can be on the table in a trice. And mini pizzas topped with canned fish, using ciabatta or pitta bread as the base, couldn't be quicker.

Griddled halibut steaks with tomato and red pepper salsa

Fish steaks make ideal fast food and serving them with a vibrant salsa transforms plain cooked fish into an exciting dish. Being a firm-fleshed fish, halibut is well suited to cooking on a ridged cast-iron grill pan which produces attractive markings on the fish. Serve with rice, a mixed leaf salad and crusty bread.

Serves 4
4 halibut steaks, about 140 g (5 oz) each
3 tbsp extra virgin olive oil
juice of 1 small orange
1 garlic clove, crushed
1 orange, cut into wedges, to garnish

Tomato and red pepper salsa
200 g (7 oz) ripe plum tomatoes, diced
½ red pepper, seeded and diced
½ red onion, finely chopped
juice of 1 small orange
15 g (½ oz) fresh basil, chopped
1 tbsp balsamic vinegar
1 tsp caster sugar
salt and pepper

Preparation time: 15 minutes
Cooking time: 4–6 minutes

1. Place the halibut steaks in a shallow non-metallic dish. Mix together the oil, orange juice, garlic and salt and pepper to taste, and spoon over the fish steaks.

2. Combine all the salsa ingredients and season with salt and pepper to taste. Spoon into a serving bowl.

3. Heat a lightly oiled ridged cast-iron grill pan or heavy-based frying pan over a high heat. Place the fish steaks on the grill pan or in the frying pan and cook for 2–3 minutes on each side, basting from time to time with the oil mixture, until the fish will just flake easily.

4. Place the fish steaks on warm serving plates and grind over some black pepper. Garnish with wedges of orange and serve with the salsa.

Some more ideas
- Other white fish steaks such as cod, haddock, hoki or swordfish, or monkfish fillets, can be cooked in the same way.
- For a tomato and olive salsa, combine the diced tomatoes with ½ diced cucumber, 4 chopped spring onions, 45 g (1½ oz) chopped stoned green or black olives and 15 g (½ oz) chopped fresh basil. Or use 1 tbsp drained and rinsed capers instead of olives.
- In summer, the fish can be cooked outdoors on a barbecue. Lay the steaks on a sheet of foil to prevent the delicate flesh slipping through the barbecue grid.

Each serving provides
kcal 254, **protein** 31 g, **fat** 11 g (of which saturated fat 2 g), **carbohydrate** 7.5 g (of which sugars 6.5 g), **fibre** 1 g

✓✓✓	B_1, B_6, C, niacin
✓✓	A, B_{12}, E
✓	iron, potassium

Plus points
- Red peppers are an excellent source of vitamin C and beta-carotene. Both these nutrients are considered to be powerful antioxidants that can help to protect against cancer and heart disease.
- Halibut is a good source of niacin, which has an important role to play in the release of energy inside cells. Niacin is one of the most stable vitamins, and there are little or no losses during preparation or cooking.

Chinese-style steamed plaice rolls

Here rolled up plaice fillets, flavoured with oyster sauce, ginger and spring onions, are set on a bed of the sea vegetable samphire and then steamed. They're served with a mixture of long-grain and wild rice.

Serves 4

340 g (12 oz) mixed long-grain and wild rice
4 plaice fillets, about 600 g (1 lb 5 oz) in total, skinned
2 tbsp oyster sauce
½ tsp caster sugar
3 garlic cloves, finely chopped
1 tsp finely chopped fresh root ginger
3 spring onions, thinly sliced
100 g (3½ oz) fresh samphire
1 carrot, shaved into strips using a vegetable peeler
1 tsp toasted sesame oil
1 tbsp chopped fresh coriander
sprigs of fresh coriander to garnish

Preparation and cooking time: 25 minutes

1 Add the rice to a large saucepan of cold water and bring to the boil. Reduce the heat and simmer for about 15 minutes, or cook according to the packet instructions, until tender. Drain well.

2 While the rice is cooking, cut the fish fillets in half lengthways. Arrange the strips, skinned side uppermost, on a plate and spread over the oyster sauce. Sprinkle with the sugar, half of the garlic, half of the ginger and half of the spring onions. Roll up the strips.

3 Place the samphire in a steamer and arrange the fish rolls on top. Sprinkle with the remaining chopped garlic and ginger, and add the carrot shavings. Cover and steam over a high heat for 5–6 minutes or until the fish will flake easily and the samphire is just tender.

4 Arrange the samphire and plaice rolls on plates with the carrot shavings. Drizzle with the sesame oil and sprinkle with the remaining spring onions and the chopped coriander. Garnish the rice with coriander sprigs, and serve.

Plus points
- Wild rice is not a true rice but the seeds of a North American grass. It contains more protein than ordinary rice and is rich in the essential amino acid, lysine, which is usually in short supply in most grains. Amino acids are the building blocks of protein.
- Using the green leaves of spring onions increases the beta-carotene content of the onions.

Some more ideas
- Use mixed Chinese greens, thinly sliced, or 225 g (8 oz) broccoli, cut into small florets, instead of the samphire.
- Serve the fish with fried rice rather than the long-grain and wild rice mixture. Cook 280 g (10 oz) long-grain rice in boiling water for 10–12 minutes, or according to the packet instructions, until tender. Drain. Stir-fry 1 onion, chopped, ½ red pepper, seeded and chopped, 1 stalk celery, diced, 3 garlic cloves, chopped, and 1 tsp chopped fresh root ginger in 1 tbsp groundnut oil for 2–3 minutes. Remove from the wok and set aside. Heat another 1 tbsp oil in the wok and add the rice, spreading it out in a thin layer. Cook over a moderate heat until lightly browned on one side. Turn over, add the stir-fried vegetables and stir-fry for 2 minutes. Add 2 tsp soy sauce and 55 g (2 oz) frozen peas and stir-fry for another 2 minutes. Sprinkle with chopped fresh coriander and serve.

Each serving provides

kcal 455, **protein** 32 g, **fat** 4 g (of which saturated fat 0.5 g), **carbohydrate** 78 g (of which sugars 3 g), **fibre** 1 g

✓✓✓	B_1, B_6, B_{12}, niacin, selenium
✓✓	A
✓	B_2, C, folate, calcium, copper, iron, potassium, zinc

Hake en papillote

Laying a piece of fish on a bed of greens, seasoning with a few aromatics and then sealing up tightly into a parcel is a simple and trouble-free way to cook fish. It's healthy too, as no water-soluble nutrients are lost.

Serves 4

280 g (10 oz) mixed Asian greens, such as pak choy and Chinese cabbage, chopped
4 hake steaks, about 140 g (5 oz) each
grated zest and juice of ½ small orange
3 tbsp shredded fresh basil
2 garlic cloves, finely chopped
120 ml (4 fl oz) dry white wine
1 tbsp extra virgin olive oil
½ medium-sized bulb of fennel, thinly sliced
1 carrot, cut into thin strips

Bulghur and herb pilaf

200 g (7 oz) bulghur wheat
1 tbsp extra virgin olive oil
juice of ½ lemon
1 garlic clove, finely chopped
2 tbsp shredded fresh basil
2 tbsp chopped fresh coriander
3 spring onions, sliced
salt and pepper

Preparation time: 20 minutes
Cooking time: 10 minutes

Each serving provides

kcal 417, **protein** 34 g, **fat** 10 g (of which saturated fat 1 g), **carbohydrate** 44 g (of which sugars 5 g), **fibre** 3 g

✓✓✓	A, B$_1$, C, niacin, iron
✓✓	calcium, copper, potassium
✓	B$_6$, folate

1 Preheat the oven to 240°C (475°F, gas mark 9). Cut out four 30 cm (12 in) squares of foil or baking parchment. Arrange one-quarter of the chopped Asian greens in the middle of each foil or paper square. Top with a fish steak, and sprinkle over the orange zest and juice, basil, garlic, white wine, olive oil, fennel, carrot, and salt and pepper to taste. Fold over the foil or paper to form a parcel, leaving a little air inside so the ingredients can steam, and twist the edges to seal. Set the parcels on a baking sheet. Set aside.

2 Combine the bulghur wheat with 900 ml (1½ pints) water in a large saucepan and bring to the boil. Reduce the heat to moderately low, cover and cook for 12–15 minutes or until the bulghur is just tender. Drain the bulghur if necessary.

3 While the bulghur is cooking, put the fish parcels into the oven and bake for 10 minutes. Open one of the parcels to check that the fish is cooked and will flake easily.

4 Fork through the cooked bulghur and mix in the olive oil, lemon juice, garlic, basil, coriander and spring onions. Season with salt and pepper to taste. Serve each person a fish parcel, letting them open them at the table, with the bulghur pilaf in a bowl.

Some more ideas

- Cod steaks can be used instead of the hake.
- Replace the dry white wine with orange juice.
- For salmon *en papillote*, divide 4 large tomatoes, sliced, among 4 foil or paper squares and lay 4 pieces of skinless salmon fillet, about 140 g (5 oz) each, on top. Sprinkle with 2 garlic cloves, finely chopped, 1 fresh red chilli, seeded and sliced, 4 spring onions, sliced, 3 tbsp chopped fresh coriander, ½ tsp ground cumin and 2 tbsp lemon juice. Wrap and bake for 10 minutes, and serve with the bulghur pilaf.

Plus points

- Hake is a good source of phosphorus, which together with calcium is needed for the hardening of bones and teeth.
- Bulghur wheat is produced from whole wheat grains. It is a good source of starchy carbohydrate, dietary fibre and B vitamins, as it contains the particularly nutritious outer layers of the grain.
- Pak choy is a variety of Chinese cabbage, the Oriental species of the cabbage family. Its nutritional content is similar to cabbages such as Savoy, being a particularly good source of folate and beta-carotene.

Quick-fried squid with chilli and fresh ginger

Rings of squid are briefly stir-fried with garlic, chilli and fresh colourful vegetables in this speedy supper dish. Take care not to overcook the squid as it has a tendency to toughen if cooked for too long.

Serves 4

280 g (10 oz) basmati rice
2 tbsp sunflower oil
2 fresh red chillies, seeded and thinly sliced
2 garlic cloves, crushed
4 tsp finely grated fresh root ginger
1 orange pepper, seeded and diced
200 g (7 oz) baby corn, sliced at an angle
200 g (7 oz) small broccoli florets, halved
450 g (1 lb) fresh squid rings
5 tbsp light soy sauce
10 spring onions, thinly sliced

Preparation and cooking time: 30 minutes

1 Bring a large saucepan of water to the boil, add the rice and cook for 10–12 minutes, or according to the packet instructions, until tender.

2 Meanwhile, heat the oil in a wok or heavy-based frying pan and stir-fry the chillies, garlic and ginger for 2 minutes to release their flavour. Toss in the pepper, corn and broccoli florets, and stir-fry for 3–4 minutes or until the broccoli is almost tender.

3 Add the squid and stir-fry for 1–2 minutes or until just firm and opaque. Spoon in the soy sauce and 2 tbsp water and scatter over the spring onions. Cook until bubbling, then serve immediately with the drained rice.

Some more ideas

- To make quick-fried squid with tomatoes and black bean sauce, stir-fry 3 garlic cloves, crushed, with the chillies, then add the squid and stir-fry for 1 minute. Add 8 tomatoes, seeded and chopped, and 4 tbsp chopped fresh coriander with the spring onions, then stir in 8 tbsp black bean sauce instead of the soy sauce and water. Cook the mixture until bubbling, and serve immediately.
- As an alternative to the squid, try raw tiger or king prawns, peeled. Allow 4–5 per person, and stir-fry for 3–4 minutes or until they turn bright pink.
- Egg noodles make a good accompaniment instead of the rice.

Each serving provides

kcal 453, **protein** 28 g, **fat** 9 g (of which saturated fat 1 g), **carbohydrate** 65 g (of which sugars 5 g), **fibre** 4 g

✓✓✓	B_1, B_6, B_{12}, C, E, niacin, copper, iron, selenium
✓✓	folate
✓	A, B_2, calcium, potassium, zinc

Plus points

- Squid, or calamari, is an excellent source of low-fat protein and of vitamin B_{12}.
- Broccoli is an excellent source of beta-carotene, vitamin C and vitamin E – all powerful antioxidants that help to protect the body's cells against the damaging effects of free radicals.

Scampi provençal

The ideal accompaniment to this stylish dish is a simple salad of sliced tomatoes drizzled with a little vinaigrette and served on a bed of fresh baby spinach leaves – perfect for a quick supper.

Serves 4
1 tbsp extra virgin olive oil
1 large onion, chopped
1 bulb of fennel, chopped
1 large garlic clove, crushed
1 can chopped tomatoes, about 400 g
120 ml (4 fl oz) fish stock, preferably home-made (see page 27)
½ tbsp fennel seeds
finely grated zest and juice of ½ orange
pinch of saffron threads
250 g (8½ oz) long-grain rice
400 g (14 oz) peeled raw scampi (langoustines)
salt and pepper
fresh basil leaves to garnish

Preparation and cooking time: 30 minutes

Each serving provides
kcal 377, **protein** 25 g, **fat** 4 g (of which saturated fat 0.5 g), **carbohydrate** 64 g (of which sugars 8 g), **fibre** 3 g

✓✓✓	B_1, B_6, B_{12}, niacin
✓✓	C, E, copper, iron, selenium, zinc
✓	folate, calcium, potassium

1. Heat the oil in a large non-stick frying pan with a tight-fitting lid. Add the onion, fennel and garlic and cook over a moderate heat, stirring occasionally, for 5 minutes or until softened but not browned. Add the tomatoes with their juice, the stock, fennel seeds, and orange zest and juice, and season with salt and pepper to taste. Bring to the boil, stirring, then reduce the heat to low and half cover the pan. Simmer for 12 minutes.

2. Meanwhile, crumble the saffron threads into a saucepan of boiling water. Add the rice and boil for 10–12 minutes, or according to the packet instructions, until tender.

3. Bring the tomato sauce back to the boil. Place the scampi on top of the sauce, cover the pan tightly and cook over a low heat for 3–4 minutes or until the scampi are cooked through and opaque. Do not boil the mixture or the scampi may toughen.

4. Drain the rice and divide among serving bowls. Spoon in the scampi and tomato sauce. Sprinkle with basil and serve at once.

Some more ideas
- This combination of seafood and tomatoes also makes a delicious sauce for 400 g (14 oz) wholemeal spaghetti.
- For tuna provençal, make the tomato sauce and, just before serving, stir in 2 cans tuna in spring water, about 200 g each, drained and flaked. This makes a great sauce for cooked pasta shells. Serve garnished with fresh dill.
- If you can't find scampi, you can use peeled raw tiger or king prawns, scallops or 400 g (14 oz) shellfish cocktail mix.
- Use 2 chopped courgettes instead of the fennel. Chopped green beans and red, yellow, orange or green peppers also work well in the sauce.
- For extra flavour, add a pinch of crushed dried chillies with the tomatoes. Or, stir in 3–4 diced canned anchovy fillets.

Plus points
- Called scampi in Italy, but known in Britain by their French name, langoustine, or as Dublin Bay prawns, this crustacean is a rich source of vitamin E. Vitamin E is actually a group of several related compounds which have powerful antioxidant properties.
- The vitamin C in tomatoes is concentrated in the jellylike substance surrounding the seeds. Vitamin C is an important nutrient for maintaining immunity and healthy skin.
- Fennel seeds are thought to aid digestion, and fennel tea is often recommended to ease flatulence.

Anchovy and sesame-topped tuna

Peppers, tomatoes and a touch of chilli make a zesty combination to partner tuna steaks, which are baked with a crisp topping. Tagliatelle is a good accompaniment, along with a crisp mixed salad or lightly steamed broccoli.

Serves 4
1½ tbsp extra virgin olive oil
1 large onion, thinly sliced
1 large red pepper, seeded and thinly sliced
1 large yellow pepper, seeded and thinly sliced
2 garlic cloves, finely chopped
1 can chopped tomatoes, about 400 g
1 tbsp tomato purée
1 bay leaf
½ tsp chilli purée
2 large tuna steaks, 2 cm (¾ in) thick, about 550 g (1¼ lb) in total

Anchovy and sesame topping
55 g (2 oz) fresh wholemeal breadcrumbs
1 garlic clove
4 anchovy fillets, drained
10 g (¼ oz) parsley
2 tbsp sesame seeds
2 tsp extra virgin olive oil
salt and pepper

Preparation time: 20 minutes
Cooking time: 10 minutes

1. Preheat the oven to 200°C (400°F, gas mark 6). Heat the oil in a frying pan or wide saucepan over a moderate heat and add the onion, peppers and garlic. Cover and cook, stirring frequently, for 3–4 minutes or until the onion has softened. Stir in the tomatoes and their juice, the tomato purée, bay leaf and chilli purée. Cover again and cook, stirring frequently, for about 7 minutes or until the peppers are just tender.

2. Meanwhile, make the topping. Combine all the ingredients in a blender or food processor and process until finely chopped. Alternatively, chop together the breadcrumbs, garlic, anchovies and parsley, put in a bowl and mix in the sesame seeds and oil with a fork until well combined.

3. Turn the pepper mixture into an ovenproof dish large enough to hold the fish in one layer. Season the tuna steaks and cut each one in half. Lay the 4 pieces in the dish and spoon over the topping to cover them evenly. Bake for 10 minutes or until the fish is just cooked. It will still be a little pink in the centre. If you prefer tuna more well done, cook for 1–2 minutes longer. Serve immediately.

Some more ideas
- Bake the anchovy and sesame-topped tuna on a bed of leeks and cabbage. Heat 1 tbsp extra virgin olive oil in a frying pan and add 2 large leeks, thinly sliced, and 400 g (14 oz) finely shredded young green cabbage. Sauté together until wilted, then spoon into the ovenproof dish and set the tuna on top.
- Instead of baking the tuna, you can griddle it, and serve with 400 g (14 oz) tagliatelle, cooked and tossed with the pepper and tomato mixture. Lightly oil a ridged cast-iron grill pan and heat over a high heat. Brush the tuna lightly with olive oil and season with salt and pepper to taste, then cook for about 3 minutes on each side. Serve immediately.
- If you're not fond of anchovies, simply omit them – the recipe will still be delicious.

Each serving provides
kcal 384, **protein** 39 g, **fat** 17 g (of which saturated fat 3 g), **carbohydrate** 21 g (of which sugars 13 g), **fibre** 5 g

✓✓✓	A, B_1, B_6, B_{12}, C, niacin, selenium
✓✓	E, copper, iron, potassium
✓	folate, calcium, zinc

Plus points
- Extra virgin olive oil is made from the first pressing of top grade olives from which the stones have been removed. It is green in colour, has a rich flavour and is high in monounsaturated fatty acids. These are the kinds of fat that can help to lower cholesterol levels in the blood.
- Anchovies contain calcium and phosphorus, both essential minerals for the maintenance of healthy bones and teeth. These minerals are retained in canned anchovy fillets.

Mini fish pizzas

Ciabatta rolls make an instant base for easy home-made pizzas. These are topped with a mixture of seafood – canned tuna, cooked prawns and squid rings – and are given an authentic Italian flavour with red pesto and mozzarella. Serve with a crisp green leaf and vegetable salad for a nutritious fast meal.

Serves 4
4 part-baked ciabatta rolls
4 tbsp red pesto
4 medium-sized tomatoes, each cut into 6 slices
1 can sweetcorn, about 200 g, well drained
125 g (4½ oz) mozzarella cheese, coarsely grated
1 can tuna in spring water, about 200 g, drained and flaked
100 g (3½ oz) cooked peeled prawns
100 g (3½ oz) squid rings
8 tsp extra virgin olive oil
salt and pepper
chopped parsley to garnish

Preparation time: 10 minutes
Cooking time: 10–12 minutes

1 Preheat the oven to 200°C (400°F, gas mark 6). Put a heavy baking sheet in the oven to heat up.

2 Split the rolls in half and spread the cut sides with the pesto, right to the edges. Arrange 3 slices of tomato on each half and sprinkle with the sweetcorn and grated mozzarella.

3 Divide the tuna, prawns and squid rings among the pizzas. Season with salt and pepper to taste and drizzle each pizza with 1 tsp of oil.

4 Put the pizzas on the hot baking sheet and bake for 10–12 minutes or until the cheese has just melted. Sprinkle with parsley and serve.

Some more ideas
• Use a part-baked ciabatta loaf or 2 small part-baked French sticks, split horizontally, as the base for the pizzas.
• Another fast pizza is pitta bread topped with canned sardines and mackerel. Grill 4 large pitta breads lightly on both sides, then spread one side of each with 1 tsp tomato purée. Tear up about 8 large fresh basil leaves and sprinkle these over the tomato purée. Cut 2 tomatoes into thin wedges and scatter these on top with 125 g (4½ oz) mozzarella cheese, cut into slivers. Drain a can of sardines in olive oil, about 120 g, (keep the oil) and a can of mackerel fillets in brine, about 120 g. Roughly flake the sardines and mackerel and place on the pizzas with 100 g (3½ oz) cooked peeled prawns. Season with salt and pepper to taste and drizzle 1 tsp of the reserved sardine oil over each pizza. Grill for 4–5 minutes. Garnish with more basil leaves and serve.
• Other canned fish can be used. Try anchovies, kipper fillets, sardines in tomato sauce, pilchards, crab, cockles or mussels.

Each serving provides
kcal 633, **protein** 44 g, **fat** 30 g (of which saturated fat 9 g), **carbohydrate** 50 g (of which sugars 9 g), **fibre** 3 g

✓✓✓ B_{12}, niacin, calcium, selenium
✓✓ A, B_1, B_6, E, copper, iron, zinc
✓ B_2, C, potassium

Plus points
• Prawns, like all shellfish, contain iodine, which is needed for the formation of thyroid hormones and the actual functioning of the thyroid gland.
• Canned tuna fish is a great storecupboard standby as it is so easy to use. Tuna canned in spring water or brine contains half the calories of tuna canned in oil.
• Sweetcorn provides a range of nutrients, including dietary fibre which is important to keep the digestive system functioning well.

Stir-fried scallops and prawns

For a quick and delicious treat, this Oriental seafood stir-fry is hard to beat. It requires very little oil and the seaweed and vegetables add lots of flavour and texture. Pickled ginger can be found in larger supermarkets.

Serves 4
juice of 1 lemon or 1 lime
2 tsp clear honey
2 tbsp light soy sauce
4 medium-sized scallops, about 200 g (7 oz) in total, quartered
24 peeled raw tiger prawns, about 170 g (6 oz) in total
10 g (¼ oz) dried wakame seaweed
340 g (12 oz) fine Chinese egg noodles
1 tbsp stir-fry oil, or 2 tsp sunflower oil mixed with 1 tsp toasted sesame oil
300 g (10½ oz) bean sprouts
150 g (5½ oz) pak choy, shredded
1½ tbsp pickled ginger

Preparation time: 10 minutes, plus 5 minutes marinating
Cooking time: 5–7 minutes

Each serving provides
kcal 492, **protein** 33 g, **fat** 11 g (of which saturated fat 3 g), **carbohydrate** 70 g (of which sugars 7 g), **fibre** 5 g

✓✓✓	B_1, B_{12}, niacin, iron
✓✓	folate, copper, selenium, zinc
✓	B_6, C, E, calcium, potassium

1 Mix together the lemon or lime juice, honey and 1 tbsp of the soy sauce. Pour this marinade over the scallops and prawns and set aside to marinate for about 5 minutes.

2 Meanwhile, place the wakame in a bowl, cover with 300 ml (10 fl oz) cold water and leave for 8–10 minutes to rehydrate. Place the noodles in a large mixing bowl and pour in enough boiling water to cover them generously. Leave to soak for 4 minutes, or according to packet instructions, until tender. Drain when they are ready.

3 Drain the scallops and prawns, reserving the marinade, and pat dry with kitchen paper. Heat a wok or heavy-based frying pan until very hot, then add the oil and swirl to coat the wok or pan. Add the scallops and prawns and stir-fry for 2–3 minutes or until the prawns have turned pink and the scallops are opaque. Remove the scallops and prawns from the wok and set aside.

4 Add the bean sprouts, pak choy, reserved marinade, remaining 1 tbsp soy sauce and the pickled ginger to the wok and stir-fry for 1–2 minutes.

5 Return the scallops and prawns to the wok with the well-drained wakame and stir-fry for 1 minute or until just heated through. Serve the stir-fry with the egg noodles.

Some more ideas
- Use 200 g (7 oz) queen scallops and 170 g (6 oz) cooked peeled prawns. They will need only 1–2 minutes stir-frying to cook the scallops and reheat the prawns.
- For a delicious vegetable-rich version of this dish, instead of bean sprouts and pak choy, use 200 g (7 oz) mixed Chinese vegetables, such as choy sam and Chinese cabbage, shredded, 4 spring onions, thinly sliced, 150 g (5½ oz) mange-tout or sugarsnap peas, 100 g (3½ oz) mushrooms, thinly sliced, and 1 can water chestnuts, about 220 g, drained and sliced. Omit the seaweed and pickled ginger. Serve the scallop and prawn stir-fry with boiled rice instead of noodles.

Plus points
- The sprouted seed has been used in Asia since ancient times but is a fairly new arrival to the West, made popular by Chinese and Japanese restaurants. Nutritionally the most significant change when a seed is sprouted is the increase in water content. Twice as much sprouted seed as dry seed must be eaten to provide the same amount of protein, carbohydrate and other nutrients.
- Wakame seaweed is usually sold dried and is then rehydrated with water. It contains some of the essential minerals – calcium, phosphorus, magnesium and iodine.

Classic grilled Dover sole

Few classy meals could be quicker and simpler. Dover sole is a real treat and its superb taste can be fully appreciated when it is cooked this way. New potatoes with fresh mint and baby leaf spinach complement this most elegant of fish dishes. Dover sole are usually sold skinned and cleaned.

Serves 4

4 small Dover sole, about 225 g (8 oz) each, cleaned and skinned
750 g (1 lb 10 oz) baby new potatoes, scrubbed
1 large sprig of fresh mint
40 g (1¼ oz) unsalted butter
finely grated zest and juice of 1 large lemon
450 g (1 lb) baby leaf spinach
freshly grated nutmeg (optional)
salt and pepper
sprigs of fresh mint to garnish
lemon wedges to serve

Preparation and cooking time: 30 minutes

1 Preheat the grill to high. Cut a piece of foil to fit the grill pan and lay the fish on top (depending on the size of the grill, you may have to cook the sole in 2 batches).

2 Put the potatoes in a saucepan, cover with boiling water and add the sprig of mint. Cook for about 15 minutes or until the potatoes are just tender.

3 Meanwhile, melt the butter in a small saucepan and mix in the lemon zest and juice. Season with salt and pepper. Brush the lemon butter over the fish and grill for 5–6 minutes or until the flesh close to the bone flakes easily when pierced with a knife. Carefully turn the fish over, brush again with the lemon butter and grill for a further 5–6 minutes.

4 While the fish is cooking, steam the spinach for 2–3 minutes or until just wilted. Season with salt, pepper and nutmeg to taste.

5 Drain the potatoes and put into a warmed serving dish. Add plenty of black pepper, toss gently and garnish with mint sprigs. Transfer the sole to warmed dinner plates and spoon over any cooking juices from the grill pan. Add lemon wedges and serve, with the potatoes and spinach.

Some more ideas

- Other, less expensive flat fish such as lemon sole, Torbay sole or small whole plaice are also delicious grilled with lemon butter. Allow 4–5 minutes cooking each side. Instead of spinach, serve with broccoli florets steamed for 2–3 minutes or until barely tender.
- Smooth, creamy mashed potatoes flavoured with herbs are another good accompaniment for grilled sole. Peel and cut up 900 g (2 lb) floury potatoes and cook in boiling water for 15–20 minutes or until tender. Drain thoroughly, then mash until smooth. Beat in 100 ml (3½ fl oz) hot semi-skimmed milk and 15 g (½ oz) unsalted butter. Season to taste, then mix in 3 tbsp chopped fresh herbs – a combination of parsley, chives and lovage is particularly good.

Each serving provides

kcal 412, **protein** 43 g, **fat** 13 g (of which saturated fat 6 g), **carbohydrate** 32 g (of which sugars 4 g), **fibre** 4 g

✓✓✓	A, B_1, B_6, C, folate, niacin, iron, potassium, selenium
✓✓	calcium
✓	B_2, E, copper, zinc

Plus points

- Sole is a useful source of vitamin B_{12}, which plays a critical role in the production of DNA and RNA, the genetic material in cells.
- New potatoes cooked in their skins have one-third more fibre than peeled potatoes, and the nutrients found just under the skin are preserved.

Pan-fried swordfish steaks with Mexican salad

The lively flavours of Mexico combine in this supper dish of spicy swordfish steaks paired with a salsa-style kidney bean salad based on the famous avocado dip, guacamole. Serve with boiled brown or white rice or, to carry through the Mexican theme, warm flour tortillas.

Serves 4

2 tbsp extra virgin olive oil
1 garlic clove, crushed
½ tsp ground coriander
4 swordfish steaks, about 450 g (1 lb) in total
2 avocados
6 ripe plum tomatoes, chopped
1 red onion, finely chopped
1 fresh red chilli, seeded and chopped
6 tbsp chopped fresh coriander
juice of 2 limes
1 can red kidney beans, about 400 g, drained
salt and pepper
85 g (3 oz) mixed salad leaves to garnish

Preparation time: 15 minutes
Cooking time: 6–10 minutes

1. Mix the oil with the garlic and ground coriander, and season with salt and pepper to taste. Brush this mixture over both sides of the swordfish steaks.

2. Heat a ridged cast-iron grill pan or non-stick frying pan until hot. Fry the fish steaks for 3–5 minutes on each side or until just cooked – they should still be very slightly translucent in the centre, as swordfish becomes dry if overcooked.

3. Meanwhile, make the salad. Peel, stone and chop the avocados, and mix with the tomatoes, onion, chilli, coriander and lime juice. Stir in the red kidney beans and season to taste.

4. Serve the spicy swordfish steaks with the salad and a garnish of mixed salad leaves.

Some more ideas
- To make spicy swordfish wraps, after cooking the fish, flake it into bite-sized pieces. While still hot, toss with 1 red pepper, seeded and finely shredded, and the salad, made without the beans. Add some fresh salad leaves tossed with sprigs of watercress and wrap the mixture in 8 warmed flour tortillas.
- As an alternative to swordfish, try shark steaks which are similar in appearance. They have a surprisingly soft flesh when cooked.
- Canned chickpeas make a nutty-textured alternative to red kidney beans.

Plus points
- Swordfish is an excellent source of niacin. This B vitamin is involved in the release of energy in cells.
- Avocados are rich in vitamin E, which has important antioxidant properties.
- Red kidney beans are a good source of soluble fibre. They also contain good amounts of the B vitamins B_1, B_6 and niacin.
- Fresh coriander is prescribed by herbalists as a tonic for the stomach, and both the seeds and leaves are recommended for urinary tract problems.

Each serving provides
kcal 460, **protein** 31 g, **fat** 26 g (of which saturated fat 5 g), **carbohydrate** 27 g (of which sugars 10 g), **fibre** 11 g

✓✓✓	B_1, B_6, B_{12}, niacin, selenium
✓✓	C, E, iron, potassium
✓	A, B_2, folate, calcium, copper, zinc

Main Course Fish

Everyday meals all the family will enjoy

FISH IS A POPULAR CHOICE for nutritious family meals, appealing to young and old alike, and offering lots of variety. The delicate flavour and tender texture of cod and haddock make them perennial favourites, and everyone will relish pesto fish cakes, or a crispy potato-topped fish pie with prawns and mushrooms. For white fish with a foreign flavour, sample monkfish in a delicious Thai green curry or plaice fillets Indian-style. And don't forget the oily fish, so rich in healthy fats, which are especially beneficial. Spicy grilled sardines with a nutty stuffing, or mackerel with tart gooseberry sauce and potatoes rosti, are both tempting and good for you.

Spicy grilled sardines

Sardines with a crunchy nut and watercress stuffing make a simple yet healthily balanced meal when served with spicy new potatoes and a salad. Sardines are a good buy – inexpensive, quick to cook and high in beneficial fish oils and vitamins. For speed, buy ready cleaned and scaled sardines.

Serves 4

750 g (1 lb 10 oz) baby new potatoes, scrubbed
12 sardines, about 1.5 kg (3 lb 3 oz) in total, cleaned and scaled
100 g (3½ oz) fresh wholemeal breadcrumbs
finely grated zest and juice of 1 lemon
45 g (1½ oz) pecan nuts, chopped
75 g (2½ oz) watercress, finely chopped
cayenne pepper
2 tbsp extra virgin olive oil
1 tbsp black mustard seeds
salt and pepper

Leafy orange salad

1 tbsp extra virgin olive oil
1 tbsp lemon juice
¼ tsp Dijon mustard
200 g (7 oz) mixed salad leaves
1 orange, peeled and segmented

Preparation and cooking time: 35–40 minutes

Each serving provides

kcal 612, **protein** 40 g, **fat** 32 g (of which saturated fat 6 g), **carbohydrate** 46 g (of which sugars 8 g), **fibre** 5 g

✓✓✓	B_1, B_6, B_{12}, C, niacin, iron, selenium
✓✓	folate, calcium, copper, potassium, zinc
✓	A, B_2, E

1 Put the potatoes into a large pan, cover with boiling water and cook for about 15 minutes or until just tender. Preheat the grill to high.

2 While the potatoes are cooking, cut the heads and any fins off the sardines with kitchen scissors. Mix the breadcrumbs with the lemon zest and half of the lemon juice. Add the pecans, watercress, and cayenne pepper and pepper to taste, and mix thoroughly. Using a teaspoon, pack the stuffing into the sardines so the cavities are well filled. Lay a piece of foil on the grill pan and arrange the sardines on top.

3 Mix the remaining lemon juice with ½ tbsp of the olive oil and a couple of pinches of cayenne pepper. Brush half of this mixture over the fish. Place the sardines under the grill and cook for 5 minutes or until the flesh next to the bone will flake easily. Gently turn the sardines over, brush with the remaining lemon juice mixture and grill for a further 5 minutes or until cooked through.

4 When the potatoes are ready, drain and cut them in half. Heat the remaining 1½ tbsp olive oil in the pan in which you cooked the potatoes. Add the mustard seeds and cook over a moderate heat for 30 seconds to 1 minute or until the seeds begin to pop. Add the potatoes and plenty of black pepper, and toss the potatoes to coat them thoroughly with the mustard seed mixture. Keep hot until ready to serve.

5 To prepare the salad, combine the olive oil, lemon juice and mustard in a salad bowl and season with salt and pepper to taste. Add the salad leaves and orange segments and toss gently in the dressing. Serve the sardines piping hot with the salad and potatoes.

Plus points

- Sardines are, strictly speaking, young pilchards, but the name is often used to describe the young of other fish such as sprats and herrings. Sardines contain useful amounts of iron, which is needed for red blood formation. A deficiency of iron in the diet leads to the development of anaemia.
- Pecans provide generous amounts of vitamin E and are a rich source of essential fatty acids and polyunsaturated fats.
- One of the reasons that the Mediterranean diet is thought to be so healthy is because olive oil, which is a good source of monounsaturated fat, is used for cooking rather than butter and other saturated fats.

Some more ideas
- Walnuts can be used instead of pecan nuts.
- For Mediterranean-style stuffed sardines, make the stuffing with 100 g (3½ oz) fresh wholemeal breadcrumbs, the finely grated zest of 1 lemon, 50 g (1¾ oz) mixed stoned black and green olives, roughly chopped, 1 plum tomato, finely chopped, 1 tbsp chopped fresh basil, and salt and pepper to taste. Cook the baby new potatoes as in the main recipe, then toss with 1½ tbsp olive oil, 1 small red onion, finely chopped, and plenty of black pepper.
- In the summer, these sardines are delicious cooked outdoors on a barbecue, in a special hinged fish grill.

Herbed fish crumble

This more-ish fish crumble is comfort food at its best: smoked haddock and whiting in a smooth sauce, covered with a crisp herby topping. Serve with baked jacket potatoes, baby carrots and peas.

Serves 4
200 g (7 oz) whiting fillet
200 g (7 oz) smoked haddock fillet
1 medium-sized leek, thinly sliced
300 ml (10 fl oz) semi-skimmed milk
2 bay leaves
45 g (1½ oz) butter
75 g (2½ oz) wholemeal flour
3 tbsp freshly grated Parmesan cheese
2 tbsp chopped fresh marjoram or 2 tsp dried marjoram
4 tsp cornflour
100 g (3½ oz) button mushrooms, thinly sliced
2 tbsp chopped fresh flat-leaf parsley
salt and pepper
sprigs of fresh marjoram to garnish

Preparation time: 25 minutes
Cooking time: 35–40 minutes

Each serving provides
kcal 319, **protein** 28 g, **fat** 14 g (of which saturated fat 9 g), **carbohydrate** 22 g (of which sugars 5 g), **fibre** 3 g

✓✓✓	B_1, B_6, niacin, selenium
✓✓	A, B_{12}, calcium, copper
✓	B_2, C, folate, iron, potassium, zinc

1 Preheat the oven to 190°C (375°F, gas mark 5). Put the fish in a single layer in a large saucepan or frying pan and add the leek, milk and bay leaves. Season with salt and pepper to taste. Bring just to the boil, then simmer gently for 5 minutes. Take the pan off the heat and leave to stand for about 5 minutes.

2 Meanwhile, in a bowl rub the butter into the flour with your fingertips to make fine crumbs. Stir in the cheese, marjoram and seasoning to taste.

3 Lift the fish out of the milk with a fish slice and put it onto a plate. Remove the skin and flake the flesh, discarding any bones.

4 Mix the cornflour to a smooth paste with a little water, add to the milk in the pan and bring to the boil, stirring until the sauce has thickened. Discard the bay leaves. Stir in the sliced mushrooms and cook for 1 minute. Gently stir in the flaked fish and chopped parsley and season with salt and pepper to taste.

5 Pour the fish mixture into a 1.2 litre (2 pint) shallow ovenproof dish. Spoon the crumble mixture evenly over the top. Bake for 35–40 minutes or until the top is golden. Serve at once, garnished with marjoram.

Plus points
- Milk is an excellent source of several important nutrients – protein, calcium, phosphorus (important for strong bones and teeth) and many of the B vitamins. Because these nutrients are concentrated in the non-fat part of milk, lower-fat milks actually contain more than full-fat milks.
- Mushrooms contain useful amounts of the B vitamins B_2 and niacin. They are also a good source of copper which is needed for bone growth.

Some more ideas
- Some children do not like the taste of wholemeal flour, so it's a good trick to mix it with an equal quantity of white flour.
- Make up a large batch of crumble topping and store it in a plastic box in the freezer. Then simply take out as much as you need and cook from frozen.
- For a Welsh-inspired cod crumble, poach 340 g (12 oz) cod or other firm white fish fillet in the milk with the leeks and bay leaves. Skin and flake the fish. Make the sauce, and stir in a jar of pickled cockles, about 160 g, drained and well rinsed, and 2 tbsp snipped fresh chives with the mushrooms. Top with a crumble made without the herbs and cheese, and flavoured instead with 1 tsp wholegrain mustard rubbed into the mixture with the butter.

Thai green curry with monkfish

This curry is wonderfully fragrant. Serve it with jasmine rice and a side dish of Chinese cabbage or broccoli florets stir-fried with garlic and a little soy sauce. Packs of Thai fresh spices that include lemongrass, lime leaves and galangal are available from many large supermarkets.

Serves 4
2 tbsp sunflower oil
600 ml (1 pint) fish stock, preferably home-made (see page 27)
2 tbsp fish sauce
2 tbsp sugar
280 g (10 oz) baby new potatoes, scrubbed and halved
1 red pepper, seeded and cut into strips
500 g (1 lb 2 oz) monkfish fillets, sliced across into medallions
115 g (4 oz) small sugarsnap peas
100 ml (3½ fl oz) coconut milk
juice of 1 lime
1 tbsp chopped fresh coriander to garnish

Green curry paste
2 tbsp finely grated fresh galangal
2 tsp finely chopped fresh lemongrass
4 lime leaves, shredded
6 tbsp finely chopped fresh coriander
6 shallots, very finely chopped
4 garlic cloves, crushed
1 tsp ground coriander
1 tsp ground cumin
1 fresh red chilli, seeded and finely chopped
finely grated zest of 1 lime

Preparation time: 25 minutes
Cooking time: 20 minutes

1. Mix together all the ingredients for the green curry paste and stir in 6 tbsp water. (If you have a food processor, you can save chopping time by using the machine to chop all of the paste ingredients with the water until smooth.)

2. Heat the oil in a non-stick pan. Add the curry paste and fry for 5 minutes, stirring frequently, until the water has evaporated and the shallots have softened and are starting to colour.

3. Pour the fish stock and fish sauce into the pan and stir in the sugar, potatoes and red pepper. Bring to the boil, then cover and cook for about 10 minutes or until the potatoes are almost tender.

4. Add the monkfish, sugarsnap peas and coconut milk, then cover again and cook gently for 5 minutes or until the fish will flake easily. Remove from the heat, stir in the lime juice and scatter over the coriander. Serve hot.

Each serving provides
kcal 304, **protein** 24 g, **fat** 11 g (of which saturated fat 1 g), **carbohydrate** 30 g (of which sugars 16 g), **fibre** 2 g

✓✓✓	B_1, B_6, C, calcium
✓✓	A, E, niacin
✓	B_{12}, copper, iron, potassium, zinc

Some more ideas
- To make a speedy Thai prawn curry, fry the shallots and garlic in the oil until softened, then pour in the fish stock, fish sauce and sugar. Add 2–3 tbsp ready-made green curry paste from a jar (take care as some brands can be quite fiery) and stir well. Simmer for 10 minutes. Add the sugarsnap peas and cook for 3 minutes, then add 200 g (7 oz) peeled raw tiger prawns. Cook for 1–2 minutes or until the prawns turn from grey to pink. Add the lime juice and 4 tbsp chopped fresh basil, and serve.
- Use small fresh asparagus tips in place of the sugarsnap peas.

Plus points
- Monkfish, like other white fish, is low in fat and therefore fits well into a healthy diet, particularly when used in recipes with other low-fat ingredients.
- Shallots tend to be milder and more subtle in flavour than onions. Like onions they contain some vitamin C and B vitamins.
- Fresh coconut milk is a popular drink in many parts of the world and a key ingredient in Caribbean and Asian cooking. The canned version is high in saturated fat, but lower-fat coconut milk is now available.

Cod with spicy Puy lentils

Dark green Puy lentils, grown in the south of France, have a unique, peppery flavour that is enhanced by chilli. They do not disintegrate during cooking and their texture is a perfect complement for the flakiness of fresh cod. Serve this satisfying dish with warm crusty bread and a mixed salad.

Serves 4

2 tbsp extra virgin olive oil
1 onion, chopped
2 celery sticks, chopped
2 medium-sized leeks, chopped
1–2 fresh red chillies, seeded and finely chopped
170 g (6 oz) Puy lentils, rinsed and drained
750 ml (1¼ pints) vegetable stock
1 sprig of fresh thyme
1 bay leaf
juice of 1 lemon
pinch of cayenne pepper
4 pieces of skinless cod fillet or cod steaks, about 140 g (5 oz) each
salt and pepper
lemon wedges to serve

Preparation and cooking time: about 35 minutes

1 Preheat the grill to moderately high. Heat 1 tbsp of the olive oil in a saucepan, add the onion, celery, leeks and chillies, and cook gently for 2 minutes. Stir in the lentils. Add the vegetable stock, thyme and bay leaf and bring to the boil. Lower the heat and simmer for about 20 minutes or until the lentils are tender. If at the end of this time the lentils have not absorbed all the stock, drain them (you can use the excess stock to make a soup).

2 While the lentils are cooking, mix together the remaining 1 tbsp oil, the lemon juice and cayenne pepper. Lay the cod in the grill pan, skinned side up, season with salt and pepper, and brush with the oil mixture. Grill for 6–7 minutes or until the fish will flake easily. There is no need to turn the fish over.

3 Spread the lentils in a warmed serving dish and arrange the pieces of cod on top. Serve immediately, with lemon wedges.

Some more ideas

- For cod with mustard lentils, cook the lentils as in the main recipe, omitting the chillies. Mix 125 g (4½ oz) fromage frais or crème fraîche with 1–2 tbsp Dijon mustard and stir into the cooked lentils. Spread a thin layer of Dijon mustard over the seasoned cod, drizzle with olive oil and grill. Serve the cod on top of the lentils, garnished with grilled cherry tomatoes.
- Hake, halibut, salmon or hoki can be used instead of cod.

Each serving provides

kcal 324, **protein** 38 g, **fat** 7.5 g (of which saturated fat 1 g), **carbohydrate** 26 g (of which sugars 6 g), **fibre** 7.5 g

✓✓✓ B_1, B_6, niacin, selenium
✓✓ B_{12}, C
✓ A, E, folate, iron, potassium

Plus points

- White fish such as cod is low in calories. Frying it in batter more than doubles the calorie content, whereas brushing it with a little oil and grilling it keeps the fat and therefore calories at healthy levels.
- Lentils, which are small seeds from a variety of leguminous plants, are classified as pulses, but unlike other pulses they do not need to be soaked before cooking. Lentils are a good source of protein, starch, dietary fibre and B vitamins. Iron absorption from lentils is poor, but vitamin C-rich foods, such as the lemon juice in this recipe, can improve this process considerably.
- Thyme has been used as an antiseptic since Greek and Roman times.

Smoked haddock kedgeree

Kedgeree, a traditional Anglo-Indian dish of rice and smoked fish, is perfect for brunch, lunch or a light supper. It is also tasty cool as a salad. Serve with seeded wholegrain bread or warm naan bread.

Serves 4

280 g (10 oz) skinless smoked haddock fillet
1 bay leaf
1 sprig of fresh thyme
2 tsp extra virgin olive oil
300 g (10½ oz) basmati rice
1 onion, finely chopped
¼ tsp garam masala
¼ tsp ground coriander
½ tsp curry powder
225 g (8 oz) shelled fresh peas or frozen peas
4 tomatoes, halved
3 tbsp finely chopped parsley
2 spring onions, finely chopped
2 hard-boiled eggs, quartered
salt and pepper
sprigs of parsley to garnish

Preparation time: 10 minutes
Cooking time: 40 minutes

Each serving provides
kcal 462, **protein** 28 g, **fat** 7 g (of which saturated fat 1.5 g), **carbohydrate** 72 g (of which sugars 6 g), **fibre** 4 g

✓✓✓	B_1, B_6, B_{12}, niacin
✓✓	A, C, iron, selenium
✓	E, folate, calcium, potassium, zinc

1 Put the haddock in a saucepan, cutting into pieces to fit, if necessary. Cover with boiling water and add the bay leaf and thyme. Cook the fish, covered, over a low heat for 8–10 minutes or until it will flake easily (the water should just simmer). Remove the fish using a fish slice and set aside. Reserve the cooking liquid.

2 Heat the oil in a large saucepan over a moderate heat. Add the rice and stir to coat thoroughly, then cook, stirring frequently, for 2 minutes. Add the onion, garam masala, coriander and curry powder, and continue cooking for 2–3 minutes, stirring, until the onion starts to soften. Add 600 ml (1 pint) of the reserved cooking liquid together with the bay leaf and thyme. Reduce the heat to moderately low, cover and simmer for 12 minutes. Add the peas, cover again and continue cooking for 10–12 minutes or until the rice is tender.

3 Meanwhile, preheat the grill to high. Place the tomatoes, cut side up, on a baking sheet and grill for 2–3 minutes or until lightly coloured and heated through.

4 Flake the fish and gently fold it into the rice with the parsley and spring onions. Season with salt and pepper to taste and transfer to a warm serving dish. Add the egg quarters, garnish with parsley sprigs and serve with the grilled tomatoes.

Plus points
- Peas, like other legumes such as lentils, soya beans and chickpeas, are a good source of protein. Peas are also rich in fibre, some of which is in the soluble form which can help to regulate blood sugar and cholesterol levels in our bodies.
- Eggs provide high-quality protein as well as zinc, vitamins A, D and E and B vitamins. Although eggs contain cholesterol, the health risks of eating eggs have often been exaggerated. Normally, dietary cholesterol has little effect on blood cholesterol levels. It is the intake of saturated fat that affects blood cholesterol.

Some more ideas
- For a fruity flavour, stir 55 g (2 oz) raisins or sultanas into the rice with the fish.
- Use brown basmati rice instead of white and cook for about 20 minutes before adding the peas.
- Add 100 g (3½ oz) sautéed sliced mushrooms with the flaked fish.
- Make a mixed seafood kedgeree. Use 150 g (5½ oz) smoked haddock and add 170 g (6 oz) cooked mussels or oysters. If using freshly cooked mussels, about 450 g (1 lb) in the shell, use the mussel cooking juices as part of the liquid to cook the rice. Canned and drained mussels or oysters can also be added. Another idea is to use 140 g (5 oz) each smoked

haddock and poached or steamed skinless fresh haddock or cod fillet.

- For a delicious herby salmon and rice dish, replace the smoked haddock with diced or flaked hot-smoked salmon fillet (no need to cook it first) or with poached salmon. Omit the spices and cook the rice in fish stock or water. Skin and chop the tomatoes instead of grilling them, and fold into the cooked rice with the salmon and parsley, plus 1 tbsp chopped fresh dill or tarragon and 1 tbsp snipped fresh chives. Instead of the hard-boiled eggs, fold in 1 peeled and diced avocado, if you wish. This dish is particularly good in the summer served at cool room temperature.
- Omit the grilled tomatoes and serve the kedgeree with a salad made from diced cucumber and halved cherry tomatoes.

Salmon with tarragon mayonnaise

Salmon is readily available all year round and is keenly priced, making it an affordable treat. This dish can be served warm or cold, with a green leaf salad tossed with mange-tout or green beans, and some crusty bread.

Serves 4
4 salmon steaks or pieces of fillet, about 125 g (4½ oz) each
150 ml (5 fl oz) dry white wine
1–2 bay leaves
strip of pared lemon zest
Tarragon mayonnaise
4 tbsp mayonnaise
150 g (5½ oz) plain low-fat yogurt
finely grated zest of 1 lemon
2 tbsp chopped fresh tarragon
Couscous
250 g (8½ oz) couscous
4 tomatoes, roughly chopped
3 spring onions, chopped
55 g (2 oz) watercress, roughly chopped
1 tbsp extra virgin olive oil
juice of 1 lemon
salt and pepper

Preparation and cooking time: 35 minutes

1 Place the salmon in a deep-sided, non-stick frying pan. Pour over the wine and add the bay leaves, lemon zest and seasoning to taste. Bring to the boil, then reduce the heat, cover and poach the salmon for 5–6 minutes or until just cooked – it should still be very slightly translucent in the centre.

2 Meanwhile, stir together the mayonnaise, yogurt, grated lemon zest and tarragon. Season with salt and pepper to taste and spoon the mixture into a serving bowl.

3 When the fish is cooked, drain off most of the cooking liquid into a measuring jug and add enough boiling water to make 360 ml (12 fl oz). Cover the pan with a lid to keep the salmon warm, off the heat.

4 Pour the diluted fish stock over the couscous in a bowl and leave for 3–4 minutes for the liquid to be absorbed. Fluff up the couscous with a fork and stir in the chopped tomatoes, spring onions and watercress. Drizzle over the olive oil and lemon juice, and stir to blend everything together. Season with salt and pepper to taste.

5 Serve the warm salmon with the couscous salad and the tarragon mayonnaise.

Each serving provides
kcal 562, **protein** 32 g, **fat** 29 g (of which saturated fat 5 g), **carbohydrate** 39 g (of which sugars 6 g), **fibre** 1 g

✓✓✓	B_1, B_6, B_{12}, E, niacin, iron
✓✓	A, C, selenium
✓	B_2, folate, calcium, potassium, zinc

Plus points
• Combining mayonnaise with plain low-fat yogurt makes a lighter sauce that is lower in calories and fat than mayonnaise alone.
• Couscous, made from semolina, is the staple food in many North African countries. It is low in fat and high in starchy carbohydrate.

Some more ideas
• If you like the aniseed flavour of Pernod, poach the salmon in 100 ml (3½ fl oz) water or stock mixed with 4 tbsp Pernod or pastis. The Pernod flavour works well with the tarragon in the mayonnaise.
• Soured cream, crème fraîche (reduced-fat if you like) and Greek-style yogurt can all be used for making the sauce in place of the yogurt and mayonnaise.
• For a watercress sauce, replace the tarragon with 30 g (1 oz) chopped watercress.
• For a special occasion, cook a whole salmon and serve it garnished with twists of lemon and sprigs of fresh tarragon. To cook salmon, season and wrap loosely in a large sheet of lightly oiled foil, then bake in a preheated 180ºC (350ºF, gas mark 4) oven, allowing 10 minutes per 450 g (1 lb). A 2–2.5 kg (4½–5½ lb) whole salmon will serve about 10 people as part of a buffet, so make triple the quantities given here for the tarragon mayonnaise and couscous.

Mackerel with gooseberry sauce

Mackerel is a well-flavoured, highly nutritious fish and is good simply grilled and served with a fruity sauce – here gooseberry and fennel, flavoured with elderflower cordial. A side dish of rosti potatoes and a green vegetable complete the meal. Ask the fishmonger to clean the fish and remove the heads if you wish.

Serves 4

3 medium-sized potatoes, about 600 g (1 lb 5 oz) in total
3 medium-sized sweet potatoes, about 600 g (1 lb 5 oz) in total
40 g (1¼ oz) unsalted butter
4 mackerel, about 170 g (6 oz) each, cleaned and trimmed
juice of ½ lemon
1 tsp extra virgin olive oil
300 g (10½ oz) fresh or frozen gooseberries
50 g (1¾ oz) bulb of fennel, finely chopped
2 tbsp concentrated elderflower cordial
salt and pepper

Preparation and cooking time: 50 minutes

Each serving provides
kcal 722, **protein** 38 g, **fat** 37 g (of which saturated fat 11 g), **carbohydrate** 62 g (of which sugars 14 g), **fibre** 8 g

✓✓✓ A, B_1, B_6, B_{12}, C, niacin, potassium, selenium
✓✓ E, copper, iron
✓ B_2, folate, calcium, zinc

1 Preheat the oven to 220°C (425°F, gas mark 7). Peel the potatoes and sweet potatoes, then coarsely grate them into a large mixing bowl. Season with salt and pepper to taste and mix thoroughly.

2 Put half the butter in a round 25 cm (10 in) ovenproof dish or tin. Heat in the oven for 1–2 minutes or until the butter starts to bubble, then remove. Turn the grated potatoes into the hot dish and press down firmly to make an even, compact cake. Dot with the remaining butter, then return to the oven and bake for 25 minutes or until dark golden brown and the centre feels soft when pierced with a skewer.

3 Meanwhile, preheat the grill to high. Season the fish with salt and pepper and make 4–5 slashes on each side. Cut a piece of foil to fit the grill pan and lay the fish on top. Mix the lemon juice with the oil and brush half over the fish. Grill for 4–5 minutes or until the flesh next to the bone will flake easily. Carefully turn the fish over, brush with the remaining lemon juice and oil mixture, and grill for a further 4–5 minutes.

4 While the fish is cooking, make the sauce. Put the gooseberries, fennel, elderflower cordial and 75 ml (2½ fl oz) water into a non-aluminium saucepan and bring to the boil. Reduce the heat and simmer gently, stirring frequently, for 5 minutes or until all the gooseberries have popped and feel tender. Taste the sauce – it should have a pleasant sour tang. If it tastes too sweet, add a squeeze of lemon juice; if too acidic, add a small splash more of elderflower cordial. Keep the sauce hot until ready to serve.

5 When the fish and potatoes are cooked, transfer the fish to a large serving platter or warmed dinner plates. Pour the sauce into a sauce boat and serve with the fish and rosti.

Plus points
- All oily fish must be eaten fresh as they spoil rapidly. The expression 'holy mackerel' comes from the days when a special licence was given to markets in Cornwall to sell the catch of the day on a Sunday.
- Gooseberries are a good source of vitamin C. Because of the high acidity of the fruit, the vitamin C is preserved when they are cooked.
- Columbus brought the sweet potato to Europe from his first voyage to the New World. Sweet potatoes have more vitamin E than any other vegetable and also provide good amounts of vitamin C and potassium.

Some more ideas

• Many children prefer fish without bones. An easy solution is to ask the fishmonger to remove the head of the fish, then slit along the back, open out the fish and remove the bones and the guts, leaving a large flat piece of boneless fish. Grill as in the main recipe.

• The boned mackerel can also be stuffed. To make an apple and fennel stuffing, combine 100 g (3½ oz) fresh wholemeal breadcrumbs, 1 medium dessert apple, cored and finely chopped, 2 tbsp finely chopped bulb of fennel, 2 tbsp finely chopped celery, the grated zest of 1 lemon and a good pinch of fresh or dried thyme. Add a beaten egg and a little salt and pepper and stir until thoroughly mixed. Spoon the stuffing on one half of each fish, then fold over the other side of the fish to re-form the fish shape. Arrange the mackerel on the foil, brush with the lemon juice mixture and grill as in the main recipe.

Pesto fish cakes

Fish cakes are popular with all the family and are a great way to encourage children to eat fish or to tempt fussy eaters. These cakes are easy to make and can be prepared ahead, then chilled until ready to cook. Serve with oven-baked tomatoes, home-made oven chips and some green vegetables.

Serves 4

400 g (14 oz) potatoes, peeled and cubed
375 g (13 oz) white fish fillets, such as cod or haddock
100 ml (3½ fl oz) semi-skimmed milk
3 spring onions, finely chopped
finely grated zest of 1 lemon
2½ tbsp pesto
30 g (1 oz) plain flour
1 large egg, beaten
85 g (3 oz) fresh wholemeal breadcrumbs
30 g (1 oz) Parmesan cheese, freshly grated
8 tomatoes, halved
salt and pepper
sprigs of fresh flat-leaf parsley to garnish

Preparation time: 40 minutes, plus cooling
Cooking time: 20 minutes

Each serving provides
kcal 405, **protein** 32 g, **fat** 14 g (of which saturated fat 5 g), **carbohydrate** 39 g (of which sugars 8 g), **fibre** 5 g

✓✓✓	B_1, B_6, B_{12}, C, niacin, selenium
✓✓	A, E, calcium, iron, potassium, zinc
✓	B_2, folate, copper

1. Place the potatoes in a saucepan, cover with boiling water and cook gently for 15 minutes or until tender.

2. Meanwhile, place the fish in a deep-sided non-stick frying pan, pour over the milk and add seasoning to taste. Bring almost to boiling point, then reduce the heat, cover and poach the fish gently for 5–6 minutes or until it will flake easily. Remove the fish and flake the flesh, discarding the skin and any bones. Reserve the milk.

3. Drain the potatoes and mash or crush with a fork. Add the fish to the potatoes with the spring onions, lemon zest, pesto and 2 tbsp of the poaching milk to make a soft mixture. Season with salt and pepper to taste. Allow the mixture to cool.

4. Shape the fish mixture into 8 thick flat cakes and dust on both sides with the flour. Place the egg on a plate and combine the breadcrumbs and Parmesan on another plate. Coat the fish cakes in the egg and then the crumbs. Chill until ready to cook.

5. Preheat the oven to 190°C (375°F, gas mark 5). Place the fish cakes on a non-stick baking sheet. Arrange the halved tomatoes on the baking sheet and sprinkle with pepper. Bake for 20 minutes. Serve the fish cakes and baked tomatoes garnished with parsley.

Some more ideas

- For a storecupboard version, instead of white fish use 2 cans of tuna in spring water or salmon, about 200 g each, well drained. Replace the pesto with 2–3 tbsp chopped parsley and a dash of Tabasco, and add 2 tbsp semi-skimmed milk.

- Home-made oven chips make a good accompaniment. Scrub 675 g (1½ lb) baking potatoes and cut into thick chips. Toss in a polythene bag with 1 tbsp sunflower oil and seasoning to taste, to coat the chips lightly. Heat a baking sheet in the oven preheated to 200°C (400°F, gas mark 6). Spread the chips in a single layer on the hot baking sheet and bake for 20 minutes. Stir and turn them over, then bake for a further 40 minutes or until tender, crisp and browned, turning occasionally.

Plus points

- 'Fish and chips' is normally a high fat meal. By baking rather than frying fish cakes and chips, the fat content is kept healthily low.
- Both cod and haddock are excellent sources of iodine, needed for the synthesis of thyroid hormones which regulate many diverse body functions. Sea fish and seaweed are the only reliable natural sources of iodine.

main course fish

118

Haddock with parsley sauce

When made with the freshest fish and parsley, this simple supper dish is a real winner. Served with mashed potatoes mixed with leeks and courgettes and a salad, it is a satisfying meal that all the family will enjoy.

Serves 4

4 pieces of haddock fillet, about 140 g (5 oz) each
20 g (¾ oz) parsley
1 small onion, thinly sliced
1 carrot, thinly sliced
6 black peppercorns
300 ml (10 fl oz) semi-skimmed milk
750 g (1 lb 10 oz) potatoes, peeled and cut into chunks
1 large leek, thinly sliced
2 courgettes, cut into thin sticks
25 g (scant 1 oz) butter
25 g (scant 1 oz) plain flour
finely grated zest and juice of ½ lemon
salt and pepper
chopped parsley to garnish
lemon wedges to serve

Preparation and cooking time: 45–50 minutes

Each serving provides

kcal 389, **protein** 36 g, **fat** 8 g (of which saturated fat 4 g), **carbohydrate** 46 g (of which sugars 9 g), **fibre** 5 g

✓✓✓	A, B_1, B_6, B_{12}, C, niacin, selenium
✓✓	folate, iron, potassium
✓	B_2, E, calcium, copper, zinc

1. Put the fish in a large frying pan. Tear the leaves from the parsley stalks and add the stalks to the pan with the onion, carrot, peppercorns and milk. Bring just to the boil, then cover and simmer very gently for 5 minutes. Remove the pan from the heat and leave for 5 minutes to complete the cooking.

2. Meanwhile, put the potatoes in a saucepan, cover with boiling water and simmer for 15 minutes or until tender. About 5 minutes before the end of the cooking time, add the white part of the leek to the potatoes. Also, set a colander on top of the pan and steam the courgettes with the green part of the leek over the potatoes.

3. Transfer the fish to a plate and remove the skin. Keep warm. Strain the cooking liquid and reserve.

4. Melt the butter in a medium-sized saucepan, stir in the flour and cook for 1 minute. Gradually stir in the cooking liquid and bring to the boil, stirring until the sauce is thickened and smooth. Finely chop the parsley leaves and stir into the sauce with the lemon zest. Season to taste and keep hot.

5. Drain the potatoes and white leeks and mash with the lemon juice and seasoning. Stir in the green leek tops and courgettes. Transfer the fish fillets to serving plates and spoon over the sauce. Garnish with parsley and serve with the mash and lemon wedges.

Some more ideas

- Make a haddock and spinach gratin. Cook the fish and potatoes as above. Slice 3 tomatoes and arrange in a shallow 1.7 litre (3 pint) flameproof dish. Steam 280 g (10 oz) spinach leaves until wilted, then squeeze dry and sprinkle with 1 tbsp lemon juice. Spread over the tomatoes and arrange the fish on top. Pour over the parsley sauce and spread over the mashed potatoes. Sprinkle with 3 tbsp grated Cheddar cheese and grill for 5 minutes or until the top is golden.
- Smoked haddock or fresh cod fillets can be used instead of haddock.

Plus points

- Courgettes provide niacin and vitamin B_6. It is the tender skins that contain the greatest concentration of these nutrients.
- Parsley was used in Greek times for its medicinal purposes, but the Romans used it as a herb and were responsible for introducing it into this country. Parsley is rich in nutrients, particularly vitamin C. Just a teaspoon of chopped parsley can make a significant contribution to the daily requirement for vitamin C.

Sole goujons with tartare dip

These strips of lemon sole are coated in breadcrumbs and baked until golden and crisp on the outside and deliciously tender in the middle. They're served with a tangy tartare dip – the perfect accompaniment for any simply cooked fish dish. New potatoes and a baby plum tomato and basil salad are ideal side dishes.

Serves 4
450 g (1 lb) lemon sole or plaice fillets, skinned
3 tbsp plain flour
1 large egg, beaten
75 g (2½ oz) fine fresh white breadcrumbs
2 tbsp sesame seeds
1 tbsp extra virgin olive oil
salt and pepper

Tartare dip
3 tbsp crème fraîche
3 tbsp mayonnaise
1 tsp Dijon mustard
4 midget gherkins, finely chopped
1 tbsp bottled capers, drained and chopped
2 tbsp chopped parsley
1 tbsp lemon juice

Preparation time: 20 minutes
Cooking time: 10 minutes

1 Preheat the oven to 220°C (425°F, gas mark 7). Using scissors or a sharp knife, cut the fish fillets across into strips about 6 x 2 cm (2½ x ¾ in).

2 Season the flour and spread on a plate. Put the egg on another plate, and mix the breadcrumbs with the sesame seeds on a third plate. Toss the fish strips in the seasoned flour, shaking off any excess, then dip each strip into the egg and, finally, coat all over with the crumbs.

3 Brush a large non-stick baking sheet with the olive oil and lay the fish strips on the sheet in one layer. Bake for 5 minutes. Turn the strips over and bake for a further 5 minutes or until the goujons are crisp and pale golden.

4 Meanwhile, make the tartare dip. Stir all the ingredients together and spoon into 4 small bowls. Serve the goujons with the tartare dip.

Some more ideas
- For home-made fish fingers, cut 550 g (1¼ lb) thick cod loin (skinless, boneless cod) into 12 strips that are 2.5 cm (1 in) thick and about 7.5 cm (3 in) long. Coat the strips with the seasoned flour, egg and crumbs and arrange on an oiled baking sheet in one layer. Drizzle a little olive oil over each strip and bake for 10–15 minutes or until golden and the fish flakes easily. Serve with the tartare dip.
- Make a watercress dip. Blend together 150 g (5½ oz) Greek-style yogurt, 2 tbsp mayonnaise, 45 g (1½ oz) chopped watercress, a large pinch of cayenne pepper and 1 tbsp lemon juice.

Each serving provides
kcal 398, **protein** 26 g, **fat** 23.5 g (of which saturated fat 6 g), **carbohydrate** 22 g (of which sugars 1.5 g), **fibre** 1.5 g

✓✓✓	B_1, B_{12}, niacin, selenium
✓✓	E, iron
✓	B_6, calcium, copper, potassium, zinc

Plus points
- Sole is a useful source of potassium, essential for the regulation of body fluids. Potassium cannot be stored in the body, so daily losses must be replaced by eating foods that provide this mineral.
- Bread is a good source of starchy carbohydrate. At least half the calories in a healthy diet should come from starchy foods.

Baked trout with cucumber sauce

Orange and lemon slices add a great flavour to this simple recipe for baked fish, and a cucumber and yogurt sauce provides a refreshing contrast. New potatoes are roasted in the oven with the fish.

Serves 4

750 g (1 lb 10 oz) new potatoes, quartered lengthways
1 tbsp extra virgin olive oil
4 small trout, about 280 g (10 oz) each, cleaned
4 sprigs of fresh tarragon
1 orange, cut into 8 slices
1 lemon, cut into 8 slices
4 tbsp orange juice
100 g (3½ oz) watercress to garnish

Cucumber sauce

200 g (7 oz) cucumber
150 g (5½ oz) plain low-fat yogurt
2 tbsp chopped fresh mint
salt and pepper

Preparation and cooking time: 40 minutes

1. Preheat the oven to 200°C (400°F, gas mark 6) and put 2 baking sheets in the oven to heat up. Put the potatoes in a large saucepan and pour over enough boiling water to cover them. Bring back to the boil, then simmer for 5 minutes. Drain and return to the pan.

2. Drizzle the oil over the potatoes and toss them quickly to coat. Spread them out on one of the hot baking sheets and roast for 10 minutes. Turn the potatoes over and roast for another 10 minutes, then turn them again and roast for a further 5 minutes or until crisp and tender.

3. Meanwhile, season inside the fish and tuck in the sprigs of tarragon. Cut out 4 squares of foil, each large enough to wrap up a fish. Cut the orange and lemon slices in half. Divide half the orange and lemon slices among the foil squares, lay the fish on top and cover with the remaining fruit slices. Sprinkle 1 tbsp orange juice over each fish.

4. Wrap up the foil to enclose the fish completely, twisting the ends to seal. Lay the parcels on the second hot baking sheet and bake for 20 minutes.

5. While the fish and potatoes are cooking, make the sauce. Grate the cucumber, put it into a sieve and press to squeeze out the water. Mix together the cucumber, yogurt and mint, and season with salt and pepper to taste.

6. Arrange the fish, orange and lemon slices and roasted potatoes on warm plates. Add a garnish of watercress and serve with the cucumber sauce.

Some more ideas

- For a very speedy trout dish, buy fillets of trout, 2 per person. Sprinkle with a little extra virgin olive oil and grill, skin side down, for 2–4 minutes, depending on the thickness (there is no need to turn them). Serve with boiled small new potatoes.
- Vary the flavour of the sauce by adding 1 tsp horseradish relish. Or, instead of mint, use 1 tbsp chopped fresh chives or green olives.
- Flavour the fish with fennel fronds, fresh coriander or parsley sprigs rather than tarragon.
- Mackerel can be used instead of trout.

Each serving provides

kcal 440, **protein** 43 g, **fat** 13 g (of which saturated fat 3 g), **carbohydrate** 40 g (of which sugars 12 g), **fibre** 3.5 g

✓✓✓	B_1, B_6, B_{12}, C, niacin, potassium
✓✓	E, calcium, iron, selenium
✓	A, B_2, folate, copper, zinc

Plus points

- Like other oily fish, trout contains beneficial fats from the omega-3 family of essential fatty acids. These help to protect the body against strokes and heart disease.
- Plain yogurt is often used as an alternative to cream. This has the advantage of helping to lower the fat content of a recipe. In addition, yogurt provides more calcium than cream on a weight for weight basis.
- Cucumbers are very refreshing due to their high water content (96%). The skin contains beta-carotene.

Prawn gumbo

A bowl of steaming gumbo – a thick and spicy cross between a soup and a stew, full of peppers, tomatoes, okra, herbs and prawns – brings you all the good tastes of the Louisiana bayou. Serve with steamed rice or crusty bread so you can enjoy all the sauce.

Serves 4

1 tbsp extra virgin olive oil
2 onions, chopped
1 red pepper, seeded and chopped
2 celery sticks, chopped
3 garlic cloves, chopped
75 g (2½ oz) lean smoked back bacon rashers, rinded and diced
1 tbsp plain flour
1 tbsp paprika
1 litre (1¾ pints) fish stock, preferably home-made (see page 27)
1 tsp chopped fresh thyme
1 can chopped tomatoes, about 225 g
2 tbsp chopped parsley
2 bay leaves
2 tsp Worcestershire sauce
Tabasco sauce to taste
100 g (3½ oz) okra, sliced crossways
340 g (12 oz) peeled raw prawns
55 g (2 oz) fine green beans, cut into bite-sized lengths
salt and pepper
3 spring onions, thinly sliced, to garnish

Preparation time: 25 minutes
Cooking time: 40 minutes

1 Heat the oil in a large saucepan, add the onions, pepper and celery, and cook for 5–6 minutes or until lightly browned. Stir in the garlic and bacon and cook for a further 3–4 minutes. Stir in the flour, increase the heat slightly and cook for 2 minutes, stirring. Stir in the paprika and cook for 2 more minutes. Gradually add the stock, stirring well to dissolve the flour mixture.

2 Add the thyme, tomatoes with their juice, parsley, bay leaves and Worcestershire sauce. Bring to the boil, then reduce the heat to a simmer and add Tabasco sauce to taste. Add the okra and simmer for 15 minutes or until the okra is tender and the gumbo mixture has thickened.

3 Add the prawns and green beans and cook for 3 minutes or until the prawns turn pink and the beans are tender. Remove the bay leaves and season the gumbo with salt and pepper to taste. Serve in bowls, sprinkled with spring onions.

Some more ideas
- Try a gumbo with the flavours of Trinidad. Instead of lean bacon, use 75 g (2½ oz) lean smoked sausage such as kabanos. In step 2, add 1 tsp chopped fresh root ginger, ½ tsp Angostura bitters, 1 small can red kidney beans, about 200 g, drained, and 1 tbsp dark rum with the tomatoes and other ingredients. Replace half the parsley with fresh coriander.
- Use a mixture of 170 g (6 oz) prawns and 170 g (6 oz) canned crab meat, adding the crab at the very end, with the final seasoning.

Plus points
- Okra contains a mucilaginous substance that is useful to thicken the liquid in dishes such as this (the name gumbo comes from the African word for okra). The nutrient content of okra is very similar to other green vegetables in that it provides useful amounts of dietary fibre, potassium, calcium, folate and vitamin C.
- Bacon is a good source of vitamin B_1, which is essential for maintaining a healthy nervous system.

Each serving provides
kcal 206, **protein** 23 g, **fat** 6 g (of which saturated fat 1 g), **carbohydrate** 17 g (of which sugars 10 g), **fibre** 4 g

✓✓✓	B_1, B_6, B_{12}, C, niacin
✓✓	A, E, iron, potassium
✓	folate, calcium, copper, selenium, zinc

Fish and mushroom pie

A simple fish pie can be transformed into a feast by the addition of prawns and mushrooms. Serve with a colourful medley of steamed vegetables, such as sugarsnap peas, carrots and baby corn.

Serves 4

550 g (1¼ lb) potatoes, peeled and cut into chunks
4 tbsp Greek-style yogurt or fromage frais
15 g (½ oz) butter
1 small onion, sliced
400 g (14 oz) piece of haddock fillet
500 ml (17 fl oz) semi-skimmed milk
2 bay leaves
4 parsley stalks
85 g (3 oz) small pasta shells
3 tbsp cornflour
½ tsp mustard powder
freshly grated nutmeg
125 g (4½ oz) cooked peeled prawns
85 g (3 oz) mushrooms, thinly sliced
3 tbsp chopped parsley
salt and pepper

Preparation time: 40 minutes
Cooking time: 20 minutes

Each serving provides

kcal 490, protein 39 g, fat 11 g (of which saturated fat 6 g), carbohydrate 62 g (of which sugars 9 g), **fibre 3 g**

✓✓✓ B_1, B_6, B_{12}, niacin
✓✓   C, calcium, copper, potassium, selenium, zinc
✓   A, B_2, folate, iron

1. Preheat the oven to 180°C (350°F, gas mark 4). Put the potatoes into a saucepan, cover with boiling water and cook for 15–20 minutes or until tender. When the potatoes are done, drain them well and mash with the yogurt or fromage frais; keep hot.

2. While the potatoes are cooking, melt the butter in a flameproof casserole, add the onion and cook gently for 5 minutes or until soft. Place the haddock on top, pour over 400 ml (14 fl oz) of the milk and add the bay leaves and parsley stalks. Cover and poach in the oven for 15 minutes or until the fish will flake easily.

3. Cook the pasta in a saucepan of boiling water for 10 minutes, or according to the packet instructions, until barely tender. Drain and set aside.

4. Put the cornflour and mustard into a saucepan, add the remaining milk and mix to a smooth paste. Strain the poaching milk from the fish into the saucepan, reserving the onion, and add nutmeg to taste. Stir well and bring to the boil, stirring. Reduce the heat and simmer for 5 minutes or until thick.

5. Flake the haddock, discarding the skin and any bones. Stir the haddock, reserved onion, prawns, mushrooms, drained pasta shells and chopped parsley into the sauce, and season with salt and pepper to taste. Return the mixture to the casserole.

6. Spoon the mashed potatoes over the fish mixture, spreading the potato evenly, right to the edge of the dish. Fork up the surface. Bake for about 20 minutes or until bubbling and browned. Serve hot.

Some more ideas

• Make a fish and vegetable pie. Omit the prawns, and add 115 g (4 oz) cooked diced carrot, 115 g (4 oz) fresh or frozen peas and 3 tbsp chopped fresh parsley to the sauce with the haddock and other ingredients. Top with mashed potato mixed with equal quantities of mashed carrots or swedes.

• Flavour the sauce with 1 tbsp anchovy essence or 2 canned anchovy fillets, drained and chopped.

Plus points

• Haddock is a useful source of vitamin B_6. This vitamin helps the body to utilise protein and it also contributes to the formation of haemoglobin, the pigment in red blood cells.
• Incorporating both potatoes and pasta in this recipe helps to boost the intake of starchy carbohydrates.
• Fromage frais is a soft cheese originating from France. The consistency varies from runny to quite thick, depending on the fat content. Plain fromage frais can be used in recipes as a low-fat alternative to cream.

Spaghetti with clams

This popular trattoria dish is easily made at home. A classic tomato sauce, flavoured with chilli and fresh herbs in true Italian style, is delicious with clams, especially if tossed with perfectly cooked spaghetti. Serve with chunks of ciabatta bread and a green salad – and a glass of red wine.

Serves 4

- 1 tbsp extra virgin olive oil
- 1 onion, chopped
- 2 garlic cloves, chopped
- 1 small fresh red chilli, seeded and chopped
- 150 g (5½ oz) chestnut mushrooms, chopped
- 1 can plum tomatoes, about 400 g
- 1 tbsp chopped fresh basil
- 1 tbsp chopped parsley
- ½ tsp sugar
- 340 g (12 oz) spaghetti
- 48 clams in their shells, about 900 g (2 lb) in total, rinsed
- 4 tbsp red or white wine

Preparation time: 15 minutes
Cooking time: 20 minutes

1. Heat the oil in a medium-sized saucepan, add the onion, garlic and chilli, and cook over a moderate heat for 5 minutes. Stir in the mushrooms and cook for 2 minutes, then add the tomatoes and their juice, crushing them down with a wooden spoon. Sprinkle in the basil, parsley and sugar and stir. Cover and simmer for 10 minutes.

2. Meanwhile, cook the spaghetti in boiling water for 10–12 minutes, or according to the packet instructions, until al dente. Drain the pasta in a colander.

3. Put the empty pasta pan back on the heat, add the clams and splash in the wine. Tip the pasta back in. Cover and cook for 3 minutes, shaking the pan occasionally. All the shells should have opened; discard any clams that remain shut.

4. Pour the tomato sauce into the spaghetti and clam mixture, and stir and toss over the heat for 1–2 minutes or until it is all bubbling. Season with salt and pepper to taste, then serve.

Plus points

- Clams are an excellent source of phosphorus. This mineral is needed for healthy bones and teeth, where up to four-fifths of the body's phosphorus is to be found.
- Contrary to popular belief, pasta – like bread and potatoes – is not a 'fattening' food. It is only when excessive amounts of oil, cream or butter are added to the accompanying sauces that the calorific value is considerably increased.
- Chestnut mushrooms tend to be larger, firmer and browner than most other cultivated mushrooms. They also have a stronger flavour. All mushrooms are a good source of copper which has many important functions, including maintaining healthy bones and helping to prevent anaemia by improving the absorption of iron from food.

Each serving provides

kcal 448, **protein** 25 g, **fat** 7 g (of which saturated fat 1 g), **carbohydrate** 73 g (of which sugars 10 g), **fibre** 6 g

✓✓✓	B_1, B_6, niacin, copper, iron
✓✓	C, folate, potassium, zinc
✓	A, E, calcium

main course fish

Some more ideas

• When fresh clams are not available, make a tomato, olive and caper sauce with canned clams. Heat 2 tsp extra virgin olive oil in a saucepan and fry 2 rashers of unsmoked back bacon, rinded and chopped. Add 1 chopped onion, 1 small red pepper, seeded and chopped, and 1 chopped garlic clove. Cook for 5 minutes, then add a can of tomatoes, about 400 g, with the juice, crushing them down. Cover and cook for 10 minutes. Stir a can of baby clams in brine, about 280 g, into the tomato sauce (with the brine), and add 8 black olives, roughly chopped, 1 tbsp capers and a handful of freshly torn basil leaves. Taste and season with black pepper. Simmer for 2 minutes, then serve the sauce over the spaghetti.

• Use plain or spinach-flavoured tagliatelle instead of spaghetti.

• Fresh cockles and mussels also work well in this dish.

Cod with a gremolata crust

Here's a delicious recipe for jazzing up plain cod fillets. Gremolata is an Italian mixture of parsley, lemon zest and garlic (and sometimes chopped anchovy). This recipe uses the gremolata with breadcrumbs to make a tasty topping for the fish, which is baked with juicy tomatoes and courgettes and served with saffron mash.

Serves 4
2 lemons
55 g (2 oz) fresh white breadcrumbs
3 tbsp chopped parsley
2 garlic cloves, crushed
4 chunky pieces of skinless cod fillet, about 550 g (1¼ lb) in total
2 tsp wholegrain mustard
3 plum tomatoes, quartered
1 large courgette, thinly sliced diagonally
1 tbsp extra virgin olive oil
900 g (2 lb) potatoes, peeled and cut into chunks
1 tsp saffron threads
3 tbsp semi-skimmed milk
salt and pepper

Preparation time: 20 minutes
Cooking time: 25 minutes

1 Preheat the oven to 200°C (400°F, gas mark 6). Finely grate the zest and squeeze the juice from 1 of the lemons. Mix the zest with the breadcrumbs, parsley and garlic, and season with salt and pepper to taste.

2 Place the cod fillets in a lightly oiled, large ovenproof dish. Spread the mustard evenly over the top of the fish, then sprinkle over the lemon juice. Arrange the tomatoes and courgette around the fish. Cut the remaining lemon into 4 wedges and put them into the dish too.

3 Spoon the breadcrumb mixture over the fish and press down lightly. Drizzle with the olive oil. Bake the fish for 25 minutes or until it will flake easily and the topping is crisp.

4 Meanwhile, place the potatoes in a saucepan, cover with boiling water and add the saffron. Cook the potatoes for 15–20 minutes or until tender. Drain the potatoes and mash with the milk. Season with salt and pepper to taste. Serve the fish with the saffron mash, tomatoes and courgettes.

Each serving provides
kcal 362, **protein** 33 g, **fat** 5 g (of which saturated fat 1 g), **carbohydrate** 48 g (of which sugars 5 g), **fibre** 5 g

✓✓✓	B_1, B_6, C, niacin, selenium
✓✓	B_{12}, folate, iron, potassium
✓	A, E, copper, zinc

Plus points
- Although wholemeal bread is thought by many people to be healthier than white bread, all breads are important in a healthy well-balanced diet. The bran and wheatgerm are removed in the milling of white flour, but iron, vitamin B_1 and niacin are added to replace these losses. Calcium is also added, and as a result white bread contains twice as much calcium as wholemeal bread – 110 mg per 100 g (3½ oz) compared to 54 mg for the same weight.
- Citrus fruits are nutritionally important for their vitamin C content.

Some more ideas
- For a special occasion, bake the cod in individual ovenproof dishes. Slice the tomatoes, and replace the courgette with 1 red or yellow pepper, seeded and chopped. Put a piece of fish in each dish and arrange the sliced tomatoes on top. Scatter over the pepper and then the breadcrumb mixture, and bake for 20 minutes. Garnish with wedges of lemon.
- For an oaty topping, replace 20 g (¾ oz) of the breadcrumbs with jumbo porridge oats.
- Pieces of skinless salmon fillet can be used instead of cod. Replace the lemon zest with orange zest and add some snipped fresh chives to the breadcrumb topping.

main course fish

Indian-style fish

Plaice fillets are flavoured with chilli, ginger, mint and coconut milk, then wrapped in parcels and baked in the oven. Courgettes tossed with mustard and sesame seeds and minted new potatoes are served alongside.

Serves 4

900 g (2 lb) baby new potatoes, scrubbed
4 plaice fillets, about 140 g (5 oz) each
2 cm (¾ in) piece fresh root ginger, finely chopped
½ red onion, finely chopped
1 fresh mild red chilli, seeded and finely chopped
4 tbsp chopped fresh mint
4 tbsp coconut milk
2 medium-sized courgettes, cut into large dice
1 tbsp sesame seeds
2 tsp yellow mustard seeds
2 tsp soy sauce
salt and pepper

Preparation and cooking time: 35–40 minutes

Each serving provides

kcal 333, **protein** 30 g, **fat** 7 g (of which saturated fat 1 g), **carbohydrate** 40 g (of which sugars 5 g), **fibre** 3 g

✓✓✓	B_1, B_6, C, niacin, selenium
✓✓	B_{12}, folate, iron, potassium
✓	A, B_2, calcium, copper, zinc

1. Preheat the oven to 180°C (350°F, gas mark 4). Put the potatoes into a medium-sized saucepan, cover with boiling water and simmer for about 15 minutes or until tender.

2. Meanwhile, cut out 4 large pieces of baking parchment or foil, each large enough to enclose a plaice fillet. Lay a fillet on each piece of paper or foil and season with salt and pepper.

3. Mix together the ginger, onion, chilli, half of the mint and the coconut milk, and spread over the fish. Fold over the paper or foil and pleat or twist the ends to seal. Put the parcels on a large baking sheet and bake for 10–12 minutes or until the fish will flake easily (open a parcel to check).

4. When the potatoes and fish are almost ready, steam the courgettes above the potatoes for 4 minutes. Heat a frying pan, add the sesame and mustard seeds, cover and fry over a moderate heat for 2–3 minutes or until lightly toasted, shaking the pan frequently.

5. Take the pan off the heat. Add the soy sauce to the seeds and quickly stir, then re-cover the pan and set aside until the seeds stop 'popping'. Stir the courgettes into the seed mixture.

6. Drain the potatoes and toss with the remaining 2 tbsp chopped mint. Arrange the fish parcels on serving plates and serve with the courgettes and the new potatoes.

Plus points
- Vitamin B_{12} is principally found in foods from animal sources or products fortified with the vitamin. Fish such as plaice, which is an excellent source of this vitamin, can be particularly useful for those who are not eating meat but are including fish in their diet.
- Baking the fish in a parcel captures all the flavour and nutrients, and the fish stays deliciously moist.

Some more ideas
- The fish parcels can be prepared earlier in the day and kept chilled until ready to cook.
- Sole or trout fillets can be cooked in the same way.
- For Indian-style salmon, use 4 pieces of salmon fillet, 115 g (4 oz) each. Instead of coconut milk, mix the juice of 2 limes with the ginger, onion, chilli and mint. Spread this over the fish, wrap and bake for 15 minutes. Use the finely grated zest from the limes to flavour 250 g (8½ oz) freshly cooked basmati rice. Also stir in 3 tbsp chopped fresh mint and 6 tbsp toasted desiccated coconut. Serve the coconut rice with the salmon.

Teriyaki swordfish brochettes

Teriyaki is a popular cooking style in Japan. It derives from teri, *meaning 'shine', and* yaki, *which means 'to grill'. The teriyaki marinade used to coat fish or meat is usually made with soy sauce, rice and sugar and can be bought ready-made from most supermarkets. It has an intense flavour, so you only need to use a little.*

Serves 4
550 g (1¼ lb) thick swordfish steaks
4 small red onions, quartered
1 large yellow pepper, seeded and cut into 16 cubes
2 limes, each cut into 8 thick slices
2 tbsp chopped fresh coriander to garnish

Marinade
3 tbsp teriyaki marinade
1 tbsp clear honey
1 tsp toasted sesame oil
1 garlic clove, crushed

Sweet chilli noodles
250 g (8½ oz) fine Chinese egg noodles
1 tbsp sunflower oil
2 garlic cloves, sliced
1 tbsp finely chopped fresh root ginger
125 g (4½ oz) mange-tout, sliced
6 spring onions, shredded
3 tbsp sweet chilli sauce
2 tbsp light soy sauce

Preparation time: 25 minutes, plus optional 30 minutes for soaking skewers
Cooking time: 8–10 minutes

1. If using wooden skewers, soak them in cold water for at least 30 minutes. Preheat the grill to high.

2. Cut the swordfish into 24 bite-sized pieces. Mix together the marinade ingredients in a bowl and toss in the fish to coat all over. Thread the fish onto 8 skewers, alternating the cubes with the onions, pepper and limes.

3. Grill the brochettes for 8–10 minutes or until the fish is just cooked but still very slightly translucent in the centre and all the ingredients are golden brown. Turn the brochettes halfway through the cooking and baste with the remaining marinade.

4. While the brochettes are cooking, prepare the noodles. Place the noodles in a saucepan of boiling water, bring back to the boil and simmer for 3 minutes. Or cook the noodles according to the packet instructions. Drain well. Heat the oil in a wok over a high heat and cook the garlic and ginger for 30 seconds. Add the mange-tout and spring onions and stir-fry for 1 minute. Add the noodles with the sweet chilli and soy sauces, and stir and toss together for 1–2 minutes.

5. Spoon the noodle mixture onto warm plates and top with the fish brochettes. Garnish with the chopped coriander and serve.

Plus points
- Swordfish is an excellent source of vitamin B_{12}, which apart from its role in the formation of red blood cells is involved in maintaining a healthy nervous system, as it helps to form the protective sheath around nerves.
- Mange-tout, meaning literally 'eat all', are a good source of vitamin C. They contain more of this vitamin than peas because the pods make an additional contribution.
- Lime is a good source of vitamin C.

Each serving provides
kcal 538, **protein** 36 g, **fat** 15 g (of which saturated fat 3 g), **carbohydrate** 69 g (of which sugars 21 g), **fibre** 5 g

✓✓✓	B_1, B_6, B_{12}, C, niacin, selenium
✓✓	iron, potassium
✓	A, B_2, E, folate, calcium, copper, zinc

Another idea

- For Italian-style monkfish brochettes, cut the 2 fillets from a 600 g (1 lb 5 oz) monkfish tail. Mix together 2 tbsp extra virgin olive oil, 2 tsp balsamic vinegar, 1 tbsp clear honey and 2 tbsp shredded fresh basil. Lay a sheet of cling film on a chopping board. Arrange 3 slices of Parma ham, trimmed of excess fat, on the cling film, overlapping them slightly, and top with a monkfish fillet. Spoon over half of the basil mixture, then wrap the fish in the ham, using the cling film to help. Repeat with the remaining monkfish fillet and 3 more slices of Parma ham. Discard the film, then use a sharp knife to cut the fish across into 2.5 cm (1 in) slices. Thread onto skewers with 12 cherry tomatoes and 1 large green pepper, seeded and diced. Brush any remaining basil mixture over the fish and vegetables. Grill for 6–8 minutes or until the fish is cooked and will flake easily. Serve with a crisp salad and crusty bread.

Especially Good

Special seafood recipes for entertaining

WHEN YOU WANT TO COOK something a bit special for a dinner party, take a look at fish and shellfish. For a chilly winter evening, what could be better than a hearty Italian seafood stew full of shellfish and vegetables and served with polenta triangles? You'll be sure to impress friends with a crispy salmon koulibiac, filo-wrapped layers of fish, rice and mushrooms. A whole sea bass flavoured with ginger, sesame and soy sauce also makes a wonderful dinner party dish. For an extra special supper, fresh chive pancakes filled with a mixture of mussels, prawns and haddock chunks poached in white wine, and topped with a cheesy sauce, will be sure to fit the bill.

Italian seafood stew

Any fish or shellfish is delicious in this Italian fisherman's stew – make the bubbling tomato mixture and add whatever is tasty and fresh from the sea. Serve with triangles of polenta grilled at the last minute.

Serves 4
2 tbsp extra virgin olive oil
1 medium-sized leek, coarsely chopped
1 onion, chopped
4 garlic cloves, chopped
½ green pepper, seeded and chopped
½ medium-sized bulb of fennel, diced
360 ml (12 fl oz) dry white wine
300 ml (10 fl oz) fish stock, preferably home-made (see page 27)
1 can chopped tomatoes, about 400 g
2 tbsp tomato purée
¼ tsp dried herbes de Provence
1 medium-sized courgette, sliced
3 tbsp coarsely chopped parsley
55 g (2 oz) shelled fresh peas or frozen peas
85 g (3 oz) baby chard or spinach leaves
200 g (7 oz) skinless cod fillet, cut into chunks
400 g (14 oz) peeled or shelled mixed shellfish, such as raw tiger or king prawns, scallops, squid rings and mussels
salt and pepper

Polenta
225 g (8 oz) instant polenta
2 tsp extra virgin olive oil

Preparation time: 20 minutes
Cooking time: 1 hour

1 Heat the oil in a large saucepan, add the leek and onion, and cook for 2 minutes or until starting to soften. Add the garlic, pepper and fennel and cook for a further 5–10 minutes or until softened.

2 Add the wine, stock and tomatoes with their juice, and season with salt and pepper to taste. Simmer for 30 minutes or until the mixture has thickened slightly. Stir in the tomato purée, herbes de Provence and courgette, and continue simmering for 10 minutes, adding a little water if the mixture becomes too thick.

3 Meanwhile, cook the polenta according to the packet instructions until it is thick. Season with salt and pepper to taste. Pour the polenta into a lightly oiled 18 x 28 cm (7 x 11 in) shallow tin. Leave until cool and firm, then cut the polenta into triangles. Preheat the grill to high.

4 Stir the parsley, peas, chard or spinach, fish and shellfish into the tomato mixture. Cover and simmer gently over a moderate heat for about 5 minutes or until all the seafood is just cooked.

5 Lightly brush the polenta triangles with the oil and grill until lightly browned. Serve the fish stew in bowls with the polenta triangles.

Plus points
- Cod provides excellent quantities of iodine. Fish is one of the most reliable sources of this essential mineral because of the consistent iodine content of sea water. Other foods depend on the iodine content of soil, which can vary considerably.
- Polenta, which is finely milled corn or maize meal, is a good gluten-free source of starchy carbohydrate.
- Fresh peas have a relatively short season, but frozen peas can be enjoyed all year round. The nutritional content of frozen peas is very similar to that of fresh as long as the recommended cooking instructions are followed – the vitamin content can be reduced by over-cooking in too much water.

Each serving provides
kcal 356, **protein** 33 g, **fat** 9 g (of which saturated fat 1 g), **carbohydrate** 22 g (of which sugars 9 g), **fibre** 5 g

✓✓✓	B_1, B_6, B_{12}, C, niacin, copper, selenium
✓✓	A, E, folate, iron, potassium, zinc
✓	calcium

especially good

Some more ideas

- Any firm white fish such as haddock or hake can be used instead of the cod.
- For an Italian clam stew with asparagus, use 3 medium-sized onions, chopped, and omit the leek and green pepper. In step 2, omit the stock. Replace the fish and shellfish with 1 kg (2¼ lb) clams in their shells. After adding them to the tomato mixture, cover and bring to the boil, then reduce the heat and simmer over a low heat for about 2 minutes or until the shells start to pop open. Add 125 g (4½ oz) thin asparagus spears, cut into bite-sized pieces, cover again and cook for a further 5 minutes or until all the clams have opened (discard any that remain shut) and the asparagus is just tender. Serve the stew with the polenta triangles or with steamed rice.

especially good

Baked whole fish with grapefruit

This colourful recipe offers an intriguing combination of citrus and fennel flavours that taste wonderful together. Serve with baked jacket potatoes and vegetables such as steamed baby carrots and marrow.

Serves 4

2 large pink grapefruit
2 tbsp extra virgin olive oil
2 large onions, halved through the stalk and sliced crossways
1 large bulb of fennel, thinly sliced
2 garlic cloves, crushed
1 tbsp fresh thyme leaves
120 ml (4 fl oz) dry white wine or vermouth
4 bay leaves
4 whole tilapia or red mullet, about 225 g (8 oz) each, cleaned
juice of 2 oranges
½ tsp chilli purée, or to taste
salt and pepper

Preparation time: 20 minutes
Cooking time: 25 minutes

Each serving provides

kcal 300, **protein** 25 g, **fat** 11 g (of which saturated fat 1 g), **carbohydrate** 23 g (of which sugars 20 g), **fibre** 5 g

✓✓✓	B_1, B_6, B_{12}, C, niacin, selenium
✓✓	potassium
✓	E, folate, calcium, copper, iron

1. Preheat the oven to 200°C (400°F, gas mark 6). Working over a bowl to catch the juices, peel the grapefruit and slice between the membranes to cut out the segments, dropping them into the bowl. Squeeze the juice from the membranes into the bowl.

2. Heat the olive oil in a large frying pan over a moderate heat. Add the onions and fennel and cook for about 4 minutes, stirring frequently, until the onion has softened and started to brown. Reduce the heat and add the garlic, thyme and wine or vermouth. Cook for 2–3 minutes, stirring frequently, until the wine has reduced by half. Season with salt and pepper to taste.

3. Turn the vegetables into an ovenproof dish large enough to hold the fish. Put a bay leaf in the cavity of each fish and season them. Lay the fish on top of the vegetables and scatter over the grapefruit segments, reserving the juice.

4. Put the grapefruit juice into a measuring jug with the orange juice. If needed, top up with water to make 300 ml (10 fl oz); if there is more juice than this, it can all be used. Stir in the chilli purée and pour the juice over the fish and vegetables. Cover with foil and bake for about 25 minutes or until the fish will flake easily. Serve hot.

Some more ideas

- Monkfish fillets can be used for this recipe instead of whole fish.
- For salmon baked on samphire, use 4 pieces of skinless salmon fillet, about 140 g (5 oz) each. Rinse 340 g (12 oz) samphire well to remove saltiness, and pick over to remove any woody stalks. Sauté 1 red onion, sliced, in 2 tbsp extra virgin olive oil until soft and golden, then mix with the samphire and turn into a baking dish. Lay the salmon fillets on top, season with pepper to taste and arrange the grapefruit segments over them. Mix together the fruit juices and chilli purée and pour over the fish. Cover with foil and bake for 20 minutes.

Plus points

- Tilapia is an excellent source of phosphorus and a good source of calcium, both minerals involved in the maintenance of healthy bones and teeth.
- Grapefruit is an excellent source of vitamin C, and pink and ruby grapefruit also contain the antioxidant beta-carotene.

especially good

Salmon koulibiac

A traditional fish dish from Russia, this is made with poached salmon, rice and mushrooms. The updated version here uses crisp filo rather than the usual puff pastry. As all the preparation can be done ahead of time, a koulibiac is an ideal dinner party dish. All it needs with it are some colourful steamed vegetables.

Serves 6

400 g (14 oz) piece of salmon fillet
3 tbsp dry white wine
1 bay leaf
6 black peppercorns
30 g (1 oz) butter
2 onions, finely chopped
200 g (7 oz) button mushrooms, thinly sliced
200 g (7 oz) basmati rice
2 tbsp finely chopped fresh dill
2 tbsp extra virgin olive oil
7 sheets filo pastry, about 200 g (7 oz) in total
1 egg, beaten
salt and pepper
lemon wedges to serve

Preparation time: 50 minutes plus 1½ hours cooling time
Cooking time: 35–40 minutes

Each serving provides

kcal 674, protein 33 g, fat 26 g (of which saturated fat 7 g), carbohydrate 77 g (of which sugars 4 g), fibre 2 g

✓✓✓	B_1, B_6, B_{12}, niacin
✓✓	E, copper, selenium
✓	B_2, folate, iron, potassium, zinc

1 Put the salmon in a non-aluminium pan with the wine, bay leaf and peppercorns. Pour in enough cold water just to cover the fish. Set the pan over a moderate heat and bring to a gentle boil. Reduce the heat so the liquid just simmers, then cover the pan and cook for 10 minutes. Remove the pan from the heat and let the fish cool in the poaching liquid.

2 Meanwhile, melt 15 g (½ oz) of the butter in a large frying pan. Add the onions and stir well, then cover and cook over a low heat for 8–10 minutes or until very soft and translucent. Add the mushrooms and season with salt and pepper to taste. Turn up the heat and cook uncovered, stirring constantly, for 5 minutes or until the mushrooms have softened. Remove the pan from the heat and leave to cool.

3 Rinse the rice and cook in a saucepan of boiling water for 10–12 minutes, or according to the packet instructions, until just tender. Drain the rice and turn it out onto a large plate or tray to cool.

4 Drain the cooled salmon and flake the flesh, discarding the skin and any bones. Gently combine the rice with the mushroom mixture. Add the chopped dill and season with salt and pepper to taste.

5 Melt the remaining 15 g (½ oz) butter in a small saucepan with the oil. Arrange 3 overlapping sheets of pastry on a lightly oiled baking sheet to make a 40 cm (16 in) square, brushing each sheet sparingly with the butter and oil mixture. Arrange 3 more sheets on top, brushing with the butter and oil.

6 Spoon half the rice mixture down the centre of the pastry to make a neat shape about 30 x 17 cm (12 x 6½ in). Top with the flaked salmon. Spoon the rest of the rice on top of the fish and mound into a neat shape. Lightly brush the edges of the pastry with beaten egg, then wrap the pastry over the filling to enclose it completely. Brush the last sheet of pastry with the remaining butter mixture, then cut into quarters. Lightly crumple each piece and secure on top of the koulibiac with a little beaten egg, to make a neat decoration. Cover and chill for up to 4 hours until ready to cook.

7 When ready to cook, preheat the oven to 200ºC (400ºF, gas mark 6). Lightly brush the koulibiac with beaten egg to glaze, then bake for 35–40 minutes or until golden brown and the centre is piping hot (check with a skewer). Transfer the koulibiac to a serving platter and add lemon wedges. Cut into slices to serve.

especially good

Plus points
• Black peppercorns are the dried fruit of a tropical vine native to India. They are picked when green and allowed to ferment in the sun before drying. Herbal practitioners believe that black pepper can have a stimulatory effect on the digestive system.
• Filo pastry is a lower-fat alternative to shortcrust and puff pastries. In 100 g (3½ oz) filo there are 2 g fat and 275 kcal; the same weight of shortcrust pastry contains 29 g fat and 449 kcal.

Another idea
• For a smoked haddock koulibiac, replace the salmon with 400 g (14 oz) smoked haddock fillet. Poach as in the main recipe, but replace the water with semi-skimmed milk. In step 2, instead of mushrooms add 125 g (4½ oz) frozen petits pois to the softened onions and cook for 1 minute. Use chopped parsley instead of dill, and add a chopped hard-boiled egg to the rice and petits pois mixture in step 4.

especially good

Seafood paella

No trip to Spain would be complete without sampling their famous rice dish, paella. The ingredients vary from region to region, but we've used monkfish, squid and mussels for this version. Serve with crusty bread.

Serves 4

large pinch of saffron threads
900 ml (1½ pints) fish stock, preferably home-made (see page 27)
400 g (14 oz) squid
2 tbsp extra virgin olive oil
200 g (7 oz) monkfish fillet, cut into bite-sized pieces
2 large garlic cloves, crushed
1 large onion, finely chopped
½ tsp paprika, or to taste
2 large red peppers, seeded and chopped
250 g (8½ oz) long-grain rice
1 can chopped tomatoes, about 225 g
150 g (5½ oz) frozen peas
12 mussels, scrubbed and beards removed
3 tbsp finely chopped parsley
salt and pepper

Preparation and cooking time: about 1 hour

Each serving provides

kcal 487, **protein** 34 g, **fat** 9 g (of which saturated fat 1.5 g), **carbohydrate** 71 g (of which sugars 11 g), **fibre** 5 g

✓✓✓ B_1, B_6, B_{12}, C, niacin, copper, selenium

✓✓ A, E, folate, iron, potassium, zinc

✓ B_2, calcium

1 Put the saffron threads in a large, wide, heavy-based pan over a moderate heat and stir constantly until they just begin to give off their aroma. Add the stock and bring to the boil. Remove the pan from the heat, cover and set aside to infuse.

2 To prepare the squid, pull the head, tentacles and insides from the bodies. Discard the head and the hard beak from the base of the tentacles. Pull out the clear quill from the bodies, and discard. Use your fingers to rub the thin grey skin from the bodies, holding them under running water. Slice the bodies into thin strips and chop the tentacles. Set aside.

3 Heat 1 tbsp of the oil in a frying pan. Add the monkfish pieces and quickly fry on all sides until lightly browned. Remove the fish and set aside. Add the remaining 1 tbsp oil to the pan. Add the garlic, onion and paprika and cook over a moderate heat for 2 minutes, stirring occasionally. Stir in the red peppers and continue cooking for about 3 minutes or until the vegetables are softened but not brown.

4 Stir in the rice so all the grains are well coated with oil. Bring the saffron-infused stock to simmering point and add half of it to the rice. Stir, then bring to the boil. Reduce the heat to low and simmer for 5 minutes or until the liquid is almost all absorbed.

5 Add the rice mixture to the stock remaining in the large pan. Gently stir in the tomatoes with their juice, the peas and monkfish pieces. Arrange the mussels on the top. Simmer for about 5 minutes. Very gently stir in the squid, then simmer for a further 15 minutes or until the rice is tender and all the liquid has been absorbed. Season with salt and pepper to taste.

6 Remove the pan from the heat, cover and leave to stand for 5 minutes. Discard any mussels that have not opened. Sprinkle the top of the paella with the parsley and serve.

Plus points

• Using the stock obtained by boiling the head, skin and bones from any white fish not only adds flavour to a dish but also some nutrients. Any vitamins and minerals that leach out into the water will make a contribution to the dish.

• Including more than one source of starchy carbohydrate at a meal is a simple way to increase intake. Serving bread with a rice dish is uncommon in this country but something that should be recommended.

Another idea

- To make a seafood risotto, in step 3, omit the paprika, and replace the red peppers with a large bulb of fennel, finely chopped. In step 4, stir in 250 g (8½ oz) risotto rice. Add 4 tbsp dry white wine and stir until it is absorbed, then add the saffron-flavoured stock, a ladleful at a time, only adding the next ladleful when the previous batch has been absorbed. Stir constantly while the rice is cooking. When about three-quarters of the stock has been added, add the browned pieces of monkfish and the squid. Omit the tomatoes, peas and mussels. Continue gradually adding the stock, stirring gently. When all the stock has been added, season to taste. Sprinkle with chopped fresh dill or parsley, cover and leave to stand off the heat for about 2 minutes before serving.

Skate with citrus-honey sauce

Poaching skate in the oven with fresh fish stock couldn't be simpler, and accompanied by a simple orange and lemon sauce, it makes a no-hassle dinner. Serve with roasted potato slices and courgettes or beans.

Serves 4

675 g (1½ lb) even-sized new potatoes, scrubbed and halved
1 tbsp extra virgin olive oil
4 pieces of skate wing, about 600 g (1 lb 5 oz) in total
250 ml (8½ fl oz) fish stock, preferably home-made (see page 27)
3 oranges
juice of 1 lemon
30 g (1 oz) butter
4 tbsp clear honey
salt and pepper
1 tbsp finely chopped parsley to garnish

Preparation and cooking time: 45 minutes

1 Preheat the oven to 200°C (400°F, gas mark 6). Put the potatoes in a roasting tin, drizzle over the oil and add salt and pepper to taste. Toss well. Roast on the top shelf of the oven for 25–30 minutes or until tender.

2 Meanwhile, arrange the skate in a single layer in a large shallow ovenproof dish and pour over the fish stock. Cover tightly with foil and poach in the oven for about 25 minutes or until the fish will flake easily.

3 While the fish and potatoes are cooking, make the sauce. Squeeze the juice from 2 of the oranges and pour into a small pan. Add the lemon juice, butter and honey. Cut the peel and pith from the remaining orange with a sharp knife. Working over the saucepan to catch the juice, cut in between the membrane to release the segments. Set the segments aside.

4 When the skate is cooked, carefully lift it from the stock and arrange on plates. Gently warm the sauce to melt the butter, but don't allow it to boil. Add the orange segments and season with salt and pepper to taste. Pour over the fish, sprinkle with the parsley and serve immediately, with the roasted potatoes.

Plus points
- An orange can provide more than twice the recommended daily intake of vitamin C. This is one of the water-soluble vitamins that cannot be stored by the body, so it is essential to eat fruit and vegetables containing vitamin C on a daily basis.
- The vitamin C content of potatoes varies with their age, dropping from 21 mg per 100 g (3½ oz) for freshly dug potatoes to 9 mg after 3 months storage.

Some more ideas
- For scallops with citrus and chive sauce, use 12 large scallops (without their corals). Heat 1 tbsp extra virgin olive oil in a large non-stick frying pan, add the scallops and sear over a high heat for about 1 minute on each side or until caramelised on the outside, but still moist inside. Keep warm while you make the sauce as in the main recipe, replacing the parsley with 1½ tbsp snipped fresh chives.
- Instead of roasted potatoes, make a wild rice and lemongrass pilaf to serve with the skate. Fry 4 chopped shallots in 1 tbsp extra virgin olive oil, then add 250 g (8½ oz) mixed long-grain and wild rice. Pour in 600 ml (1 pint) vegetable stock and stir in 1 tsp finely chopped lemongrass. Cover and simmer for 20 minutes, or according to the packet instructions, until the rice is tender and the stock has been absorbed. Add 3 tbsp chopped fresh coriander and serve.

Each serving provides

kcal 420, **protein** 28 g, **fat** 10 g (of which saturated fat 4.5 g), **carbohydrate** 58 g (of which sugars 30 g), **fibre** 4 g

✓✓✓ B_1, B_6, B_{12}, C, niacin
✓✓ potassium
✓ A, B_2, folate, calcium, copper, iron, selenium, zinc

especially good

especially good

147

Oriental sea bass

A whole fish cooked with ginger, garlic and spring onions is a traditional centrepiece in a Chinese meal. Here it is served with a mixture of noodles and bean sprouts to make a very special dish.

Serves 4

1 tsp sunflower oil
1 sea bass, about 800 g (1¾ lb), cleaned and scaled
1 lime, cut into 4 slices
6 spring onions, cut into fine shreds
1 carrot, cut into fine matchsticks
2.5 cm (1 in) piece fresh root ginger, cut into fine matchsticks
2 garlic cloves, thinly sliced
2 tbsp light soy sauce
1 tsp toasted sesame oil
1 tbsp fresh coriander leaves
fresh coriander leaves to garnish
lime halves to serve

Noodles

250 g (8½ oz) fine Chinese egg noodles
1 tbsp sunflower oil
2 small red onions, cut into very thin wedges
1 garlic clove, thinly sliced
300 g (10½ oz) bean sprouts
3 tbsp light soy sauce

Preparation time: 15 minutes
Cooking time: 30–35 minutes

Each serving provides

kcal 485, **protein** 39 g, **fat** 14 g (of which saturated fat 3 g), **carbohydrate** 55 g (of which sugars 7 g), **fibre** 4 g

✓✓✓ A, B_1, B_{12}, niacin, iron
✓✓ calcium
✓ B_6, C, E, folate, copper, potassium, zinc

1. Preheat the oven to 200°C (400°F, gas mark 6). Brush a large sheet of thick foil with the oil and place the fish on top. Place the lime slices inside the fish and scatter over the spring onions, carrot, ginger and garlic. Drizzle over the soy sauce and sesame oil, and sprinkle over the coriander leaves. Bring the ends of the foil together and fold and twist to seal in the fish. Place on a baking sheet. Bake for 30–35 minutes or until the fish will flake easily (open the parcel to check).

2. Meanwhile, place the noodles in a saucepan of boiling water, return to the boil and simmer for 3 minutes. Or cook them according to the packet instructions. Drain well. Heat the oil in a wok, add the onions and garlic, and cook over a high heat for 30 seconds. Add the bean sprouts and cook for 1 minute or until they begin to soften. Add the noodles together with the soy sauce. Cook over a high heat for 2–3 minutes, stirring and tossing well.

3. Remove the fish from the oven, unwrap and transfer to a hot serving platter. Garnish with coriander leaves and lime halves. Serve the fish cut into slices, with the noodles.

Some more ideas

- The Chinese flavours in this dish also work well with whole red mullet, which take about 20 minutes to cook.
- For Mediterranean baked sea bass, use 4 fillets, about 140 g (5 oz) each, and place on 4 oiled pieces of foil. Mix together 4 tomatoes, seeded and diced, 40 g (1½ oz) stoned black olives, quartered, 2 tbsp drained capers, roughly chopped, 1 tbsp chopped parsley, 2 tbsp extra virgin olive oil and some seasoning. Divide the mixture among the fish and wrap in the foil. Bake for 15 minutes. Meanwhile, make a salad by mixing together 1 bulb of fennel, finely shredded, 1 large courgette, sliced, and 2 red onions, cut into thin wedges. Toss with 2 tbsp lemon juice, 1 tbsp extra virgin olive oil, and seasoning to taste. Serve the fish with the salad and boiled new potatoes.

Plus points

- Eggs add flavour and colour to noodles and only a minute amount of fat. Egg noodles are an excellent source of starchy carbohydrate.
- Sunflower is one of the most popular oils, having a mild flavour. It is a particularly good source of vitamin E, which is a powerful antioxidant that protects cell membranes from damage by free radicals.

especially good

Parma-wrapped lemon sole

For this elegant dish, fillets of lemon sole are spread with a nutty herb filling, then rolled up in thin slices of Parma ham and baked with butter and white wine. Creamy mashed potatoes mixed with rocket and steamed asparagus spears are ideal accompaniments.

Serves 4

900 g (2 lb) floury potatoes, such as King Edwards, peeled and cut into large chunks
8 very thin slices Parma ham, about 125 g (4½ oz) in total, trimmed of fat
4 large lemon sole fillets, about 150 g (5½ oz) each, skinned
90 g (3¼ oz) fresh wholemeal breadcrumbs
75 g (2½ oz) chopped toasted hazelnuts
2 tbsp chopped fresh coriander
2 eggs, beaten
4 tbsp white wine
30 g (1 oz) butter
100 ml (3½ fl oz) semi-skimmed milk
2 tbsp chopped rocket
500 g (1 lb 2 oz) asparagus spears
salt and pepper

Preparation and cooking time: 45 minutes

Each serving provides

kcal 686, **protein** 52 g, **fat** 30 g (of which saturated fat 8 g), **carbohydrate** 53 g (of which sugars 6 g), **fibre** 8 g

✓✓✓	B_1, B_6, B_{12}, C, E, folate, niacin, copper, iron, potassium, selenium
✓✓	A, zinc
✓	B_2, calcium

especially good

1. Preheat the oven to 190°C (375°F, gas mark 5). Put the potatoes into a large pan and pour over boiling water to cover. Cook over a moderate heat for about 15 minutes or until tender.

2. Meanwhile, lay 2 overlapping slices of Parma ham on a board and place a fish fillet on top, skinned side up. Combine the breadcrumbs with the hazelnuts, coriander, eggs and a little pepper. Spread one-quarter of this mixture on top of the fish, pressing it over evenly. Carefully roll up the fish and ham like a swiss roll. Repeat with the remaining Parma ham, sole fillets and hazelnut filling.

3. Arrange the fish rolls in a lightly greased ovenproof dish. Pour over the wine. Using 15 g (½ oz) of the butter, put a dab on top of each roll. Cover tightly with foil and bake for 20–25 minutes or until the fish will flake easily.

4. Meanwhile, drain and mash the potatoes, then beat in the milk, remaining 15 g (½ oz) butter and the rocket, and season to taste. Transfer to a serving dish and keep hot. Steam the asparagus for about 4 minutes or until just tender.

5. Serve the fish, cut into slices, on individual warmed dinner plates, with the asparagus and potatoes.

Some more ideas

- Replace the Parma ham with 170 g (6 oz) thinly sliced smoked salmon.
- Make the filling using finely chopped parsley instead of coriander, and chopped almonds or pine nuts instead of hazelnuts, and add the grated zest of 1 lemon.
- Snipped fresh chives can be used instead of rocket in the mashed potatoes.
- Flounder or plaice fillets can be cooked in the same way.

Plus points

- The low fat content of lemon sole allows for some higher fat ingredients to be used with it, particularly in a special recipe. Even so, the saturated fat content of this dish is healthily low.
- Hazelnuts were known in China 5000 years ago, and were also eaten by the Romans. Although a particularly good source of vitamin E and most of the B vitamins, apart from B_{12}, hazelnuts contain over a third of their weight as fat. However, the major component of the fat is monounsaturated.
- Like similar dark green, leafy vegetables, rocket is a good source of the B vitamin folate and the antioxidant beta-carotene.

Turbot with sauce maltaise

Simply poached turbot is perfect with this lower-fat version of a classic hollandaise-style sauce flavoured with blood oranges. Serve with steamed new potatoes, mange-tout and baby corn.

Serves 4

300 ml (10 fl oz) fish stock, preferably home-made (see page 27)
1 shallot, sliced
1 lemon slice
1 bay leaf
6 black peppercorns, crushed
4 turbot fillets, about 140 g (5 oz) each

Sauce maltaise

85 g (3 oz) unsalted butter
1 tbsp blood orange juice
1 tbsp white wine vinegar
3 black peppercorns, lightly crushed
2 egg yolks
1 tsp lemon juice
1 tsp finely grated orange zest
125 g (4½ oz) tomatoes, skinned, seeded and finely diced
salt and pepper
fresh tarragon sprigs to garnish

Preparation and cooking time: 30 minutes

Each serving provides

kcal 331, **protein** 27 g, **fat** 24 g (of which saturated fat 13 g), **carbohydrate** 2 g (of which sugars 2 g), **fibre** 0.5 g

✓✓✓	B_1, B_{12}, niacin
✓✓	A
✓	B_6, C, E, calcium, iron, potassium

1 Place the stock, shallot, lemon slice, bay leaf and peppercorns in a pan wide enough to hold the fillets in a single layer. Bring to the boil, then remove from the heat and set aside to infuse while you make the sauce.

2 Melt the butter in a small saucepan. Pour off the clear golden liquid into a small bowl, discarding the milky sediment, and set aside to cool slightly.

3 Put the orange juice, vinegar, peppercorns and 1 tbsp water in a small saucepan and boil for 2 minutes or until reduced by half. Transfer to the top of a double boiler or a heatproof bowl set over a saucepan of simmering water. The base of the pan or bowl should not touch the water.

4 Whisk in the egg yolks and continue whisking for 4–5 minutes or until the mixture thickens and becomes pale. Gradually whisk in the melted butter, drop by drop. Continue whisking after all the butter has been incorporated, until the sauce is thick enough to hold a ribbon trail on the surface when the whisk is lifted – this will take 4–5 minutes.

5 If at any point the sauce begins to curdle, immediately remove it from the heat, add an ice cube and whisk briskly until it comes together again. Remove the ice cube, return to the heat and continue whisking in the butter.

6 Stir in the lemon juice and orange zest and season with salt and pepper to taste. Remove the saucepan or double boiler from the heat. Stir in the tomatoes, then cover and set aside while you poach the fish.

7 Strain the cooled fish stock and return it to the pan. Add the fish fillets – the liquid should just cover the fillets; if there is too much, spoon it off and reserve to use in fish soups. Slowly increase the heat so the stock just simmers but doesn't boil, and poach the fish fillets for about 5 minutes, depending on the thickness, until they will flake easily.

8 Remove the fillets with a fish slice, gently shaking off any excess liquid, and set on warmed plates. Spoon over the sauce, garnish with tarragon sprigs and serve.

Plus points

- Turbot is an excellent source of niacin, needed to release energy from carbohydrate foods.
- Tomatoes contain lycopene, a valuable antioxidant. Recent studies suggest that lycopene may help to protect against bladder and pancreatic cancers.

Some more ideas

- Turbot is an expensive fish. For a more economical version, you can use 8 skinned sole fillets, about 70 g (2¼ oz) each, poaching them as in the main recipe.
- Instead of the sauce maltaise, serve the fish with a fresh orange and tomato salsa. Halve and finely chop 200 g (7 oz) mixed red and yellow cherry tomatoes. Peel and segment 2 oranges, and chop the segments. Toss the oranges and tomatoes together. Season with salt and pepper to taste, and sprinkle over 2 tbsp finely chopped fresh herbs, such as tarragon, parsley and chives. Stir gently, then cover and chill until required.
- The poaching liquid can be cooled and stored in the fridge for up to 1 day to use as the base of a fish soup.

Seafood and chive pancakes

A richly flavoured sauce complements seafood wrapped in chive pancakes in this healthy version of a classic dish. Serve with broccoli florets or another green vegetable.

Serves 4
30 g (1 oz) butter
2 shallots, finely chopped
1 kg (2¼ lb) mussels, scrubbed and beards removed
4 tbsp white wine
1 bay leaf
200 g (7 oz) skinless haddock fillet, cut into 2 cm (¾ in) chunks
30 g (1 oz) plain flour
150 ml (5 fl oz) semi-skimmed milk
1 tbsp chopped fresh dill or chives
100 g (3½ oz) cooked peeled prawns
50 g (1¾ oz) Gruyère cheese, finely grated
30 g (1 oz) fresh breadcrumbs
salt and pepper
sprigs of fresh dill to garnish

Chive pancakes
100 g (3½ oz) plain flour
2 eggs
300 ml (10 fl oz) semi-skimmed milk
2 tbsp snipped fresh chives
1 tsp extra virgin olive oil

Preparation time: 40 minutes
Cooking time: 20 minutes

Each serving provides
kcal 445, **protein** 35 g, **fat** 18 g (of which saturated fat 9 g), **carbohydrate** 40 g (of which sugars 6 g), **fibre** 2 g

✓✓✓ B_1, B_{12}, niacin, calcium, iron, selenium
✓✓ A, B_6, zinc
✓ B_2, E, folate, copper, potassium

1 To make the pancakes, sift the flour and a good pinch of salt into a bowl, add the eggs and half of the milk, and mix well with an electric hand mixer for 2 minutes or until the batter is smooth with bubbles rising to the surface. Alternatively, you can use a whisk, which will take a bit longer. Stir in the remaining milk and the chives.

2 Heat an 18–20 cm (7–8 in) non-stick frying pan. Add a little oil, then pour in enough batter to coat the bottom of the pan. Cook over a moderate heat until golden brown on the base, then flip the pancake over and cook the other side briefly. Remove from the pan to a plate.

3 Repeat with the rest of the batter, adding a little more oil every so often, to make 8 pancakes in all. Stack the pancakes on the plate, interleaving them with kitchen paper.

4 Melt one-third of the butter in a large, deep saucepan and cook the shallots for 2 minutes. Add the mussels, wine and bay leaf, cover tightly and cook over a fairly high heat for 3 minutes, shaking the pan a few times. Drain the mussels in a colander set over a bowl to catch the juices. Discard any mussels that have not opened. Remove the mussels from the shells and set them aside in a bowl (there should be about 200 g/7 oz mussels); discard the shells and the bay leaf.

5 Strain the cooking juices through a fine sieve and pour back into the large pan. Bring to a simmer, then add the haddock chunks and poach for 2 minutes. Remove the haddock pieces with a draining spoon and add them to the mussels. Reserve the cooking liquid.

6 Preheat the oven to 200°C (400°F, gas mark 6). Melt the remaining butter in a small saucepan, stir in the flour and cook for 1 minute. Whisk in the reserved cooking liquid and the milk. Bring almost to the boil, then simmer for 3–4 minutes, stirring, until thickened and smooth. Add the dill or chives and season with salt and pepper to taste. Pour 150 ml (5 fl oz) of the sauce into the bowl of seafood. Add the prawns and stir gently to mix.

7 Lay out all the pancakes and divide the fish mixture among them. Fold the pancakes into triangles. Spoon a little of the remaining sauce into 4 individual gratin dishes, or into a large shallow, ovenproof dish, just to cover the bottom. Arrange the filled pancakes in the dishes, overlapping them slightly, then pour the remaining sauce over the top and sprinkle with the cheese and breadcrumbs. Bake for 20 minutes or until the sauce is bubbling and the top is golden brown. Garnish with dill sprigs and serve.

Plus points
- Mussels contain useful amounts of zinc, which is a mineral found in all tissues of the body. Zinc is necessary for the functioning of the immune system and therefore protection against infections.
- Like most cheeses, Gruyère is a good source of calcium, essential for healthy teeth and bones, plus zinc which has an important role to play in wound healing.
- Including milk in recipes as well as in drinks can help to ensure an adequate intake of calcium.

Some more ideas
- Use the seafood mixture to fill large flour tortillas (you'll need 1 tortilla per person, and can just roll them up). Or try it as a filling in a fish lasagne.
- A mixture of skinless salmon and haddock fillet or cod with smoked haddock also works well in the filling.

especially good

A glossary of nutritional terms

Antioxidants These are compounds that help to protect the body's cells against the damaging effects of free radicals. Vitamins C and E, beta-carotene (the plant form of vitamin A) and the mineral selenium, together with many of the phytochemicals found in fruit and vegetables, all act as antioxidants.

Calorie A unit used to measure the energy value of food and the intake and use of energy by the body. The scientific definition of 1 calorie is the amount of heat required to raise the temperature of 1 gram of water by 1 degree Centigrade. This is such a small amount that in this country we tend to use the term kilocalories (abbreviated to *kcal*), which is equivalent to 1000 calories. Energy values can also be measured in kilojoules (kJ): 1 kcal = 4.2 kJ.

A person's energy (calorie) requirement varies depending on his or her age, sex and level of activity. The estimated average daily energy requirements are:

Age (years)	Female (kcal)	Male (kcal)
1–3	1165	1230
4–6	1545	1715
7–10	1740	1970
11–14	1845	2220
15–18	2110	2755
19–49	1940	2550
50–59	1900	2550
60–64	1900	2380
65–74	1900	2330

Carbohydrates These energy-providing substances are present in varying amounts in different foods and are found in three main forms: sugars, starches and non-starch polysaccharides (NSP), usually called fibre.

There are two types of sugars: *intrinsic sugars*, which occur naturally in fruit (fructose) and sweet-tasting vegetables, and *extrinsic sugars*, which include lactose (from milk) and all the non-milk extrinsic sugars (NMEs) – sucrose (table sugar), honey, treacle, molasses and so on. The NMEs, or 'added' sugars, provide only calories, whereas foods containing intrinsic sugars also offer vitamins, minerals and fibre. Added sugars (*simple carbohydrates*) are digested and absorbed rapidly to provide energy very quickly. Starches and fibre (*complex carbohydrates*), on the other hand, break down more slowly to offer a longer-term energy source (see also Glycaemic Index). Starchy carbohydrates are found in bread, pasta, rice, wholegrain and breakfast cereals, and potatoes and other starchy vegetables such as parsnips, sweet potatoes and yams.

Healthy eating guidelines recommend that at least half of our daily energy (calories) should come from carbohydrates, and that most of this should be from complex carbohydrates. No more than 11% of our total calorie intake should come from 'added' sugars. For an average woman aged 19–49 years, this would mean a total carbohydrate intake of 259 g per day, of which 202 g should be from starch and intrinsic sugars and no more than 57 g from added sugars. For a man of the same age, total carbohydrates each day should be about 340 g (265 g from starch and intrinsic sugars and 75 g from added sugars).

See also Fibre and Glycogen.

Cholesterol There are two types of cholesterol – the soft waxy substance called blood cholesterol, which is an integral part of human cell membranes, and dietary cholesterol, which is contained in food. *Blood cholesterol* is important in the formation of some hormones and it aids digestion. High blood cholesterol levels are known to be an important risk factor for coronary heart disease, but most of the cholesterol in our blood is made by the liver – only about 25% comes from cholesterol in food. So while it would seem that the amount of cholesterol-rich foods in the diet would have a direct effect on blood cholesterol levels, in fact the best way to reduce blood cholesterol is to eat less saturated fat and to increase intake of foods containing soluble fibre.

Fat Although a small amount of fat is essential for good health, most people consume far too much. Healthy eating guidelines recommend that no more than 33% of our daily energy intake (calories) should come from fat. Each gram of fat contains 9 kcal, more than twice as many calories as carbohydrate or protein, so for a woman aged 19–49 years this means a daily maximum of 71 g fat, and for a man in the same age range 93.5 g fat.

Fats can be divided into 3 main groups: saturated, monounsaturated and polyunsaturated, depending on the chemical structure of the fatty acids they contain. *Saturated fatty acids* are found mainly in animal fats such as butter and other dairy products and in fatty meat. A high intake of saturated fat is known to be a risk factor for coronary heart disease and certain types of cancer. Current guidelines are that no more than 10% of our daily calories should come from saturated fats, which is about 21.5 g for an adult woman and 28.5 g for a man.

Where saturated fats tend to be solid at room temperature, the *unsaturated fatty acids* – monounsaturated and polyunsaturated – tend to be liquid. *Monounsaturated fats* are found predominantly in olive oil, groundnut (peanut) oil, rapeseed oil and avocados. Foods high in *polyunsaturates* include most vegetable oils – the exceptions are palm oil and coconut oil, both of which are saturated.

Both saturated and monounsaturated fatty acids can be made by the body, but certain polyunsaturated fatty acids – known as *essential fatty acids* – must be supplied by food. There are 2 'families' of these essential fatty acids: *omega-6*, derived from linoleic acid, and *omega-3*, from linolenic acid. The main food sources of the omega-6 family are vegetable oils such as olive and sunflower; omega-3 fatty acids are provided by oily fish, nuts, and vegetable oils such as soya and rapeseed.

When vegetable oils are hydrogenated (hardened) to make margarine and reduced-fat spreads, their unsaturated fatty acids can be changed into trans fatty acids, or '*trans fats*'. These artificially produced trans fats are believed to act in the same way as saturated fats within the body – with the same risks to health. Current healthy eating guidelines suggest that no more than 2% of our daily calories should come from trans fats, which is about 4.3 g for an adult woman and 5.6 g for a man. In thinking about the amount of trans fats you consume, remember that major sources are processed foods such as biscuits, pies, cakes and crisps.

Fibre Technically non-starch polysaccharides (NSP), fibre is the term commonly used to describe several different compounds, such as pectin, hemicellulose, lignin and gums, which are found in the cell walls of all plants. The body cannot digest fibre, nor does it have much nutritional value, but it plays an important role in helping us to stay healthy.

Fibre can be divided into 2 groups – soluble and insoluble. Both types are provided by most plant foods, but some foods are particularly good sources of one type or the other. *Soluble fibre* (in oats, pulses, fruit and vegetables) can help to reduce high blood cholesterol levels and to control blood sugar levels by slowing down the absorption of sugar. *Insoluble fibre* (in wholegrain cereals, pulses, fruit and vegetables) increases stool bulk and speeds the passage of waste material through the body. In this way it helps to prevent constipation, haemorrhoids and diverticular disease, and may protect against bowel cancer.

Our current intake of fibre is around 12 g a day. Healthy eating guidelines suggest that we need to increase this amount to 18 g a day.

Free radicals These highly reactive molecules can cause damage to cell walls and DNA (the genetic material found within cells). They are believed to be involved in the development of heart disease, some cancers and premature ageing. Free radicals are produced naturally by the body in the course of everyday life, but certain factors, such as cigarette smoke, pollution and over-exposure to sunlight, can accelerate their production.

Gluten A protein found in wheat and, to a lesser degree, in rye, barley and oats, but not in corn (maize) or rice. People with *coeliac disease* have a sensitivity to gluten and need to eliminate all gluten-containing foods, such as bread, pasta, cakes and biscuits, from their diet.

Glycaemic Index (GI) This is used to measure the rate at which carbohydrate foods are digested and converted into sugar (glucose) to raise blood sugar levels and provide energy. Foods with a high GI are quickly broken down and offer an immediate energy fix, while those with a lower GI are absorbed more slowly, making you feel full for longer and helping to keep blood sugar levels constant. High-GI foods include table sugar, honey, mashed potatoes and watermelon. Low-GI foods include pulses, wholewheat cereals, apples, cherries, dried apricots, pasta and oats.

Glycogen This is one of the 2 forms in which energy from carbohydrates is made available for use by the body (the other is *glucose*). Whereas glucose is converted quickly from carbohydrates and made available in the blood for a fast energy fix, glycogen is stored in the liver and muscles to fuel longer-term energy needs. When the body has used up its immediate supply of glucose, the stored glycogen is broken down into glucose to continue supplying energy.

Minerals These inorganic substances perform a wide range of vital functions in the body. The *macrominerals* – calcium, chloride, magnesium, potassium, phosphorus and sodium – are needed in relatively large quantities, whereas much smaller amounts are required of the remainder, called *microminerals*. Some microminerals (selenium, magnesium and iodine, for example) are needed in such tiny amounts that they are known as *'trace elements'*.

There are important differences in the body's ability to absorb minerals from different foods, and this can be affected by the presence of other substances. For example, oxalic acid, present in spinach, interferes with the absorption of much of the iron and calcium spinach contains.
• *Calcium* is essential for the development of strong bones and teeth. It also plays an important role in blood clotting. Good sources include dairy products, canned fish (eaten with their bones) and dark green, leafy vegetables.
• *Chloride* helps to maintain the body's fluid balance. The main source in the diet is table salt.
• *Chromium* is important in the regulation of blood sugar levels, as well as levels of fat and cholesterol in the blood. Good dietary sources include red meat, liver, eggs, seafood, cheese and wholegrain cereals.

• *Copper*, component of many enzymes, is needed for bone growth and the formation of connective tissue. It helps the body to absorb iron from food. Good sources include offal, shellfish, mushrooms, cocoa, nuts and seeds.
• *Iodine* is an important component of the thyroid hormones, which govern the rate and efficiency at which food is converted into energy. Good sources include seafood, seaweed and vegetables (depending on the iodine content of the soil in which they are grown).
• *Iron* is an essential component of haemoglobin, the pigment in red blood cells that carries oxygen around the body. Good sources are offal, red meat, dried apricots and prunes, and iron-fortified breakfast cereals.
• *Magnesium* is important for healthy bones, the release of energy from food, and nerve and muscle function. Good sources include wholegrain cereals, peas and other green vegetables, pulses, dried fruit and nuts.
• *Manganese* is a vital component of several enzymes that are involved in energy production and many other functions. Good dietary sources include nuts, cereals, brown rice, pulses and wholemeal bread.
• *Molybdenum* is an essential component of several enzymes, including those involved in the production of DNA. Good sources are offal, yeast, pulses, wholegrain cereals and green leafy vegetables.
• *Phosphorus* is important for healthy bones and teeth and for the release of energy from foods. It is found in most foods. Particularly good sources include dairy products, red meat, poultry, fish and eggs.
• *Potassium*, along with sodium, is important in maintaining fluid balance and regulating blood pressure, and is essential for the transmission of nerve impulses. Good sources include fruit, especially bananas and citrus fruits, nuts, seeds, potatoes and pulses.
• *Selenium* is a powerful antioxidant that protects cells against damage by free radicals. Good dietary sources are meat, fish, dairy foods, brazil nuts, avocados and lentils.
• *Sodium* works with potassium to regulate fluid balance, and is essential for nerve and muscle function. Only a little sodium is needed – we tend to get too much in our diet. The main source in the diet is table salt, as well as salty processed foods and ready-prepared foods.
• *Sulphur* is a component of 2 essential amino acids. Protein foods are the main source.
• *Zinc* is vital for normal growth, as well as reproduction and immunity. Good dietary sources include oysters, red meat, peanuts and sunflower seeds.

Phytochemicals These biologically active compounds, found in most plant foods, are believed to be beneficial in disease prevention. There are literally thousands of different phytochemicals, amongst which are the following:

• *Allicin*, a phytochemical found in garlic, onions, leeks, chives and shallots, is believed to help lower high blood cholesterol levels and stimulate the immune system.
• *Bioflavonoids*, of which there are at least 6000, are found mainly in fruit and sweet-tasting vegetables. Different bioflavonoids have different roles – some are antioxidants, while others act as anti-disease agents. A sub-group of these phytochemicals, called *flavonols*, includes the antioxidant *quercetin*, which is believed to reduce the risk of heart disease and help to protect against cataracts. Quercetin is found in tea, red wine, grapes and broad beans.
• *Carotenoids*, the best known of which are *beta-carotene* and *lycopene*, are powerful antioxidants thought to help protect us against certain types of cancer. Highly coloured fruits and vegetables, such as blackcurrants, mangoes, tomatoes, carrots, sweet potatoes, pumpkin and dark green, leafy vegetables, are excellent sources of carotenoids.
• *Coumarins* are believed to help protect against cancer by inhibiting the formation of tumours. Oranges are a rich source.
• *Glucosinolates*, found mainly in cruciferous vegetables, particularly broccoli, Brussels sprouts, cabbage, kale and cauliflower, are believed to have strong anti-cancer effects. *Sulphoraphane* is one of the powerful cancer-fighting substances produced by glucosinolates.
• *Phytoestrogens* have a chemical structure similar to the female hormone oestrogen, and they are believed to help protect against hormone-related cancers such as breast and prostate cancer. One of the types of these phytochemicals, called *isoflavones*, may also help to relieve symptoms associated with the menopause. Soya beans and chickpeas are a particularly rich source of isoflavones.

Protein This nutrient, necessary for growth and development, for maintenance and repair of cells, and for the production of enzymes, antibodies and hormones, is essential to keep the body working efficiently. Protein is made up of *amino acids*, which are compounds containing the 4 elements that are necessary for life: carbon, hydrogen, oxygen and nitrogen. We need all of the 20 amino acids commonly found in plant and animal proteins. The human body can make 12 of these, but the remaining 8 – called *essential amino acids* – must be obtained from the food we eat.

Protein comes in a wide variety of foods. Meat, fish, dairy products, eggs and soya beans contain all of the essential amino acids, and are therefore called first-class protein foods. Pulses, nuts, seeds and cereals are also good sources of protein, but do not contain the full range of essential amino acids. In practical terms, this really doesn't matter – as long as you include a variety of different protein foods in your diet, your body will get all the amino acids it needs. It is important, though, to eat protein foods every day because the essential amino acids cannot be stored in the body for later use.

The RNI of protein for women aged 19–49 years is 45 g per day and for men of the same age 55 g. In the UK most people eat more protein than they need, although this isn't normally a problem.

Reference Nutrient Intake (RNI) This denotes the average daily amount of vitamins and minerals thought to be sufficient to meet the nutritional needs of almost all individuals within the population. The figures, published by the Department of Health, vary depending on age, sex and specific nutritional needs such as pregnancy. RNIs are equivalent to what used to be called Recommended Daily Amounts or Allowances (RDA).

RNIs for adults (19–49 years)

Vitamin A	600–700 mcg
Vitamin B_1	0.8 mg for women, 1 mg for men
Vitamin B_2	1.1 mg for women, 1.3 mg for men
Niacin	13 mg for women, 17 mg for men
Vitamin B_6	1.2 mg for women, 1.4 mg for men
Vitamin B_{12}	1.5 mg
Folate	200 mcg (400 mcg for first trimester of pregnancy)
Vitamin C	40 mg
Vitamin E	no recommendation in the UK; the EC RDA is 10 mg, which has been used in all recipe analyses in this book
Calcium	700 mg
Chloride	2500 mg
Copper	1.2 mg
Iodine	140 mcg
Iron	14.8 mg for women, 8.7 mg for men
Magnesium	270–300 mg
Phosphorus	550 mg
Potassium	3500 mg
Selenium	60 mcg for women, 75 mcg for men
Sodium	1600 mg
Zinc	7 mg for women, 9.5 mg for men

Vitamins These are organic compounds that are essential for good health. Although they are required in only small amounts, each one has specific vital functions to perform. Most vitamins cannot be made by the human body, and therefore must be obtained from the diet. The body is capable of storing some vitamins (A, D, E, K and B_{12}), but the rest need to be provided by the diet on a regular basis. A well-balanced diet, containing a wide variety of different foods, is the best way to ensure that you get all the vitamins you need.

Vitamins can be divided into 2 groups: *water-soluble* (B complex and C) and *fat-soluble* (A, D, E and K). Water-soluble vitamins are easily destroyed during processing, storage, and the preparation and cooking of food. The fat-soluble vitamins are less vulnerable to losses during cooking and processing.

• *Vitamin A* (retinol) is essential for healthy vision, eyes, skin and growth. Good sources include dairy products, offal (especially liver), eggs and oily fish. Vitamin A can also be obtained from *beta-carotene*, the pigment found in highly coloured fruit and vegetables. In addition to acting as a source of vitamin A, beta-carotene has an important role to play as an antioxidant in its own right.

• **The B Complex vitamins** have very similar roles to play in nutrition, and many of them occur together in the same foods.
Vitamin B_1 (thiamin) is essential in the release of energy from carbohydrates. Good sources include milk, offal, meat (especially pork), wholegrain and fortified breakfast cereals, nuts and pulses, yeast extract and wheat germ. White flour and bread are fortified with B_1 in the UK.
Vitamin B_2 (riboflavin) is vital for growth, healthy skin and eyes, and the release of energy from food. Good sources include milk, meat, offal, eggs, cheese, fortified breakfast cereals, yeast extract and green leafy vegetables.
Niacin (nicotinic acid), sometimes called vitamin B_3, plays an important role in the release of energy within the cells. Unlike the other B vitamins it can be made by the body from the essential amino acid tryptophan. Good sources include meat, offal, fish, fortified breakfast cereals and pulses. White flour and bread are fortified with niacin in the UK.
Pantothenic acid, sometimes called vitamin B_5, is involved in a number of metabolic reactions, including energy production. This vitamin is present in most foods; notable exceptions are fat, oil and sugar. Good sources include liver, kidneys, yeast, egg yolks, fish roe, wheat germ, nuts, pulses and fresh vegetables.
Vitamin B_6 (pyridoxine) helps the body to utilise protein and contributes to the formation of haemoglobin for red blood cells. B_6 is found in a wide range of foods including meat, liver, fish, eggs, wholegrain cereals, some vegetables, pulses, brown rice, nuts and yeast extract.
Vitamin B_{12} (cyanocobalamin) is vital for growth, the formation of red blood cells and maintenance of a healthy nervous system. B_{12} is unique in that it is principally found in foods of animal origin. Vegetarians who eat dairy products will get enough, but vegans need to ensure they include food fortified with B_{12} in their diet. Good sources of B_{12} include liver, kidneys, oily fish, meat, cheese, eggs and milk.
Folate (folic acid) is involved in the manufacture of amino acids and in the production of red blood cells. Recent research suggests that folate may also help to protect against heart disease. Good sources of folate are green leafy vegetables, liver, pulses, eggs, wholegrain cereal products and fortified breakfast cereals, brewers' yeast, wheatgerm, nuts and fruit, especially grapefruit and oranges.
Biotin is needed for various metabolic reactions and the release of energy from foods. Good sources include liver, oily fish, brewers' yeast, kidneys, egg yolks and brown rice.

• *Vitamin C* (ascorbic acid) is essential for growth and vital for the formation of collagen (a protein needed for healthy bones, teeth, gums, blood capillaries and all connective tissue). It plays an important role in the healing of wounds and fractures, and acts as a powerful antioxidant. Vitamin C is found mainly in fruit and vegetables.

• *Vitamin D* (cholecalciferol) is essential for growth and the absorption of calcium, and thus for the formation of healthy bones. It is also involved in maintaining a healthy nervous system. The amount of vitamin D occurring naturally in foods is small, and it is found in very few foods – good sources are oily fish (and fish liver oil supplements), eggs and liver, as well as breakfast cereals, margarine and full-fat milk that are fortified with vitamin D. Most vitamin D, however, does not come from the diet but is made by the body when the skin is exposed to sunlight.

• *Vitamin E* is not one vitamin, but a number of related compounds called tocopherols that function as antioxidants. Good sources of vitamin E are vegetable oils, polyunsaturated margarines, wheatgerm, sunflower seeds, nuts, oily fish, eggs, wholegrain cereals, avocados and spinach.

• *Vitamin K* is essential for the production of several proteins, including prothombin which is involved in the clotting of blood. It has been found to exist in 3 forms, one of which is obtained from food while the other 2 are made by the bacteria in the intestine. Vitamin K_1, which is the form found in food, is present in broccoli, cabbage, spinach, milk, margarine, vegetable oils, particularly soya oil, cereals, liver, alfalfa and kelp.

Nutritional analyses

The nutritional analysis of each recipe has been carried out using data from *The Composition of Foods* with additional data from food manufacturers where appropriate. Because the level and availability of different nutrients can vary, depending on factors like growing conditions and breed of animal, the figures are intended as an approximate guide only.

The analyses include vitamins A, B_1, B_2, B_6, B_{12}, niacin, folate, C, D and E, and the minerals calcium, copper, iron, potassium, selenium and zinc. Other vitamins and minerals are not included, as deficiencies are rare. Optional ingredients and optional serving suggestions have not been included in the calculations.

Index

Titles in italics are for recipes in 'Some More Ideas'.

A

Anchovies 16–17, 22
 Anchovy and sesame-topped tuna 90
Apples: Fennel, apple and herring salad 74–5
Asian greens: Hake *en papillote* 84
Asparagus: *Italian clam stew with* 139
 Parma-wrapped lemon sole 150
Avocados: Crab and avocado salad 60
 Gravad lax with ginger 46

B

Bass *see* Sea bass
Beta-carotene 30, 34, 53, 62, 70, 72, 77, 80, 83, 84, 86, 122, 140, 150
Blinis, Three-fish 44–5
Bloaters 22
Bream 11
Buckling 22
Bulghur wheat: Crab and avocado salad 60
 Hake *en papillote* 84
Buying seafood 26

C

Calcium 11, 32, 60, 74, 84, 90, 95, 104, 124, 130, 140, 155, 157
Canned fish 22
Cannellini beans: *Italian cannellini bean and tuna salad* 68
 Italian-style mackerel and bean salad 75
Carbohydrates 6, 10, 54, 70, 120, 126, 138, 144, 149
Carrageen 21
Caviar 23
Cheese: Mini fish pizzas 92
 Parmesan-topped mussels 40
Chinese shrimp soup 32
Chinese-style steamed plaice rolls 83
Cholesterol 11, 18, 48, 50, 110, 156
Choux puffs, seafood 38–9
Choux ring filled with salmon and watercress 39

Clams 19, 25
 Italian clam stew with asparagus 139
 Spaghetti with clams 128–9
Cod 11, 23
 Cod with a gremolata crust 130
 Cod with mustard lentils 108
 Cod with spicy Puy lentils 108
 Fish balls 32
 Home-made fish fingers 120
 Italian seafood stew 138–9
 Pesto fish cakes 116
Cooking methods 24–5
Copper 30, 60, 104, 128, 157
Couscous: Fennel, apple and herring salad 74–5
 Salmon with tarragon mayonnaise 113
Crab 19, 25, 27
 Crab and avocado salad 60
 Crab and celeriac chowder 30
 Sesame prawn and crab toasts 54
 Tomato and crab soup 30
Crumble, Herbed fish 104
Cucumber sauce, Baked trout with 122
Curries: *Curried lime and honey dressing* 65
 Thai green curry with monkfish 106
 Thai prawn curry 106

D

Dried fish 23
Dulse 21

F

Fat 7, 16, 156
Fennel: Fennel, apple and herring salad 74–5
 Grilled oysters with fennel and spinach topping 56
 Scampi provençal 88
Fibre 10, 66, 68, 84, 98, 108, 110, 124, 156
Fish and mushroom pie 126
Fish and vegetable pie 126
Fish balls 32
Fish cakes, pesto 116
Five-spice prawn and water chestnut toasts 54
Folate 53, 62, 68, 84, 124, 150, 158
Frozen fish 22, 26
Frying 25

G

Gooseberry sauce, Mackerel with 114–15
Grapefruit, Baked whole fish with 140
Gravad lax 23
 Gravad lax with ginger 46

H

Haddock 11
 Chunky fish soup 34–5
 Fish and mushroom pie 126
 Haddock and spinach gratin 119
 Haddock with parsley sauce 119
 Thai fish cakes with dipping sauce 50–1
 see also Smoked haddock
Hake 11
 Hake *en papillote* 84
Halibut 11
 Griddled halibut steaks with tomato and red pepper salsa 80
 Oriental-style halibut salad 72
 Trio of warm seafood salad 62–3
Herbed fish crumble 104
Herrings 17, 23
 Fennel, apple and herring salad 74–5
 Three-fish blinis 44–5
Hoki 11
Hygiene 27

I, J

Indian-style fish 133
Indian-style salmon 133
Iodine 10, 11, 92, 95, 116, 138, 157
Irish moss 21
Iron 11, 40, 44, 56, 102, 108, 128, 130, 157
Italian cannellini bean and tuna salad 68
Italian clam stew with asparagus 139
Italian seafood stew 138–9
Italian-style mackerel and bean salad 75
Italian-style monkfish brochettes 135
John Dory 14

K, L

Kedgeree 110–11
Kippers 22
 Marinated kipper salad 66
 Pickled kippers 45

Koulibiac 142–3
Langoustines 19
 Scampi provençal 88
Laver 21
Lemon: Lemon mackerel pâté 43
 Lemon shells 43
Lentils: *Cod with mustard lentils* 108
 Cod with spicy Puy lentils 108
Lobster 19, 25, 27
 Lobster and papaya salad 65
 Lobster bisque 36–7
 Lobster salad with lime dressing 65
Lumpfish roe 23
 Three-fish blinis 44–5

M

Mackerel 17
 Italian-style mackerel and bean salad 75
 Mackerel with gooseberry sauce 114–15
 see also Smoked mackerel
Magnesium 95, 157
Mangoes: Prawn, melon and mango salad 77
Mayonnaise: Salmon with tarragon mayonnaise 113
Mediterranean baked sea bass 149
Mediterranean prawn and vegetable tartlets 49
Mediterranean-style stuffed sardines 103
Melon: Prawn, melon and mango salad 77
Microwaves 24–5
Middle Eastern salmon cakes 51
Monkfish 14
 Italian-style monkfish brochettes 135
 Seafood paella 144–5
 Thai green curry with monkfish 106
Mullet 14
Mushrooms: Fish and mushroom pie 126
Mussels 19–20, 25, 27
 Mixed seafood kedgeree 110
 Parmesan-topped mussels 40
 Seafood and chive pancakes 154–5
 Seafood choux puffs 38–9
 Trio of warm seafood salad 62–3

N, O

Niacin 62, 80, 98, 104, 119, 130, 152, 158
Noodles: Oriental sea bass 149
 Stir-fried scallops and prawns 95
 Sweet chilli noodles 134
Nori 21
Oily fish 10, 16–17
Okra: Prawn gumbo 124
Olives: *Tomato and olive salsa* 80
Omega-3 fatty acids 10, 12, 53, 122
Orange: *Orange and tomato salsa* 153
 Skate with citrus-honey sauce 146
 Turbot with sauce maltaise 152–3
Oriental sea bass 149
Oriental-style halibut salad 72
Oysters 20, 25
 Grilled oysters with fennel and spinach topping 56

P

Paella, seafood 144–5
Pan-frying 25
Pancakes: Seafood and chive pancakes 154–5
 Three-fish blinis 44–5
Papaya: *Lobster and papaya salad* 65
Papillote, 24
 Hake *en papillote* 84
 Indian-style fish 133
 Indian-style salmon 133
 Salmon en papillote 84
Parma-wrapped lemon sole 150
Parmesan-topped mussels 40
Pasta: *Prawn and pasta salad* 70
 Smoked trout and pasta salad 70
Pâtés: Lemon mackerel pâté 43
 Salmon and watercress pots 53
 Smoked trout pâté 43
Peppers: Griddled halibut steaks with tomato and red pepper salsa 80
 Provençal tuna and pepper salad 68
 Smoked trout and pasta salad 70
Pesto fish cakes 116

Phosphorus 10, 54, 84, 90, 95, 104, 128, 140, 157
Pickled fish 23
Pie: Fish and mushroom 126
Fish and vegetable 126
Pilaff, Wild rice and lemongrass 146
Pilchards 22
Pizzas, Mini fish 92
Plaice 14
  Chinese-style steamed plaice rolls 83
  Indian-style fish 133
Poaching 25
Polenta: Italian seafood stew 138–9
Potassium 11, 48, 65, 72, 114, 120, 124, 157
Potatoes: Baked trout with cucumber sauce 122
  Classic grilled Dover sole 96
  Cod with a gremolata crust 130
  Fish and mushroom pie 126
  Haddock and spinach gratin 119
  Haddock with parsley sauce 119
  Indian-style fish 133
  Oven chips 116
  Parma-wrapped lemon sole 150
  Pesto fish cakes 116
  Skate with citrus-honey sauce 146
  Spicy grilled sardines 102–3
  Thai fish cakes with dipping sauce 50–1
Prawns 20, 25
  Fish and mushroom pie 126
  Five-spice prawn and water chestnut toasts 54
  Mediterranean prawn and vegetable tartlets 49
  Prawn and pasta salad 70
  Prawn gumbo 124
  Prawn, melon and mango salad 77
  Sesame prawn and crab toasts 54
  Stir-fried scallops and prawns 95
  Thai prawn curry 106
Preserved fish 22–3
Protein 7, 10, 34, 54, 86, 110, 157–8
Provençal tuna and pepper salad 68

R
Reference Nutrient Intake (RNI) 158
Rice: Chinese-style steamed plaice rolls 83
  Quick-fried squid with chilli and fresh ginger 86
  Salmon koulibiac 142–3
  Scampi provençal 88
  Seafood paella 144–5
  Seafood risotto 145
  Smoked haddock kedgeree 110–11
  Wild rice and lemongrass pilaff 146
Roes 23

S
Salads 59–77
  Crab and avocado 60
  Fennel, apple and herring 74–5
  Grilled salmon 72
  Italian cannellini bean and tuna 68
  Italian-style mackerel and bean 75
  Lobster and papaya 65
  Lobster with lime dressing 65
  Marinated kipper 66
  Oriental-style halibut 72
  Pan-fried swordfish steaks with Mexican salad 98
  Prawn and pasta 70
  Prawn, melon and mango 77
  Provençal tuna and pepper 68
  Smoked trout and pasta 70
  Trio of warm seafood salad 62–3
Salmon 17, 22, 23
  Choux ring filled with salmon and watercress 39
  Gravad lax with ginger 46
  Grilled salmon salad 72
  Indian-style salmon 133
  Middle Eastern salmon cakes 51
  Salmon and watercress pots 53
  Salmon baked on samphire 140
  Salmon en papillote 84
  Salmon koulibiac 142–3
  Salmon with tarragon mayonnaise 113
  see also Smoked salmon
Salt 7
Samphire 21
  Chinese-style steamed plaice rolls 83
  Salmon baked on samphire 140
Sardines 17, 22
  Mediterranean-style stuffed sardines 103
  Spicy grilled sardines 102–3
Scallops 20, 25
  Scallops with citrus and chive sauce 146
  Seafood choux puffs 38–9
  Stir-fried scallops and prawns 95
  Trio of warm seafood salad 62–3
Scampi 19
  Scampi provençal 88
Sea bass 14
  Mediterranean baked sea bass 149
  Oriental sea bass 149
Sea vegetables 21
Seafood and chive pancakes 154–5
Seafood choux puffs 38–9
Seafood paella 144–5
Seafood risotto 145
Seakale 21
Seaweeds 21
Selenium 10, 38, 60, 65, 157
Sesame prawn and crab toasts 54
Shark 14
Shellfish 11, 18–20, 25
  Italian seafood stew 138–9
Shrimp 20, 25
  Chinese shrimp soup 32
  see also Prawns
Skate 14
  Skate with citrus-honey sauce 146
Smoked cod 22
Smoked fish 22–3
Smoked haddock 22
  Herbed fish crumble 104
  Mixed seafood kedgeree 110
  Smoked haddock kedgeree 110–11
  Smoked haddock koulibiac 143
  Smoked haddock tartlets 48–9
Smoked mackerel 23
  Lemon mackerel pâté 43
Smoked salmon 23
  Salmon and watercress pots 53
  Three-fish blinis 44–5
Smoked trout 23
  Smoked trout and pasta salad 70
  Smoked trout pâté 43
Sodium 10, 11, 157
Sole 14
  Classic grilled Dover sole 96
  Parma-wrapped lemon sole 150
  Sole goujons with tartare dip 120
Soups 29–37
  Chinese shrimp soup 32
  Chunky fish soup 34–5
  Crab and celeriac chowder 30
  Lobster bisque 36–7
  Tomato and crab soup 30
Spaghetti with clams 128–9
Spinach: Classic grilled Dover sole 96
  Grilled oysters with fennel and spinach topping 56
  Haddock and spinach gratin 119
Sprats 22
Squid 20
  Quick-fried squid with chilli and fresh ginger 86
  Quick-fried squid with tomatoes and black bean sauce 86
  Seafood paella 144–5
Steaming 25
Stir-frying 25
Stock 27
Stockfish 23
Swordfish 14
  Pan-fried swordfish steaks with Mexican salad 98
  Spicy swordfish wraps 98
  Teriyaki swordfish brochettes 134–5

T
Tartare dip 120
Tartlets, Smoked haddock 48–9
Teriyaki swordfish brochettes 134–5
Thai fish cakes with dipping sauce 50–1
Thai green curry with monkfish 106
Thai prawn curry 106
Tilapia 14
  Baked whole fish with grapefruit 140
Tomatoes: Griddled halibut steaks with tomato and red pepper salsa 80
  Quick-fried squid with tomatoes and black bean sauce 86
  Tomato and crab soup 30
  Tomato and olive salsa 80
Trout 17
  Baked trout with cucumber sauce 122
  see also Smoked trout
Tuna 17, 22
  Anchovy and sesame-topped tuna 90
  Italian cannellini bean and tuna salad 68
  Mini fish pizzas 92
  Provençal tuna and pepper salad 68
  Tuna provençal 88
Turbot 14
  Turbot with sauce maltaise 152–3

V
Vitamin A 12, 62, 72, 74, 77, 110, 158
Vitamin B complex 10, 44, 62, 66, 68, 84, 86, 96, 98, 104, 106, 108, 110, 119, 124, 126, 130, 133, 134, 150, 158
Vitamin C 11, 12, 30, 34, 43, 48, 53, 56, 62, 66, 68, 70, 80, 86, 88, 106, 108, 114, 119, 124, 130, 134, 140, 146, 158
Vitamin D 10, 12, 43, 68, 74, 110, 158
Vitamin E 12, 53, 60, 62, 86, 88, 98, 102, 110, 114, 149, 150, 158
Vitamin K 158

W, Z
Wakame 21
Watercress: Salmon and watercress pots 53
Watercress dip 120
White fish 10, 12–15
Whitebait 17
Whiting 14
  Herbed fish crumble 104
Wild rice and lemongrass pilaff 146
Zinc 11, 44, 56, 60, 110, 155, 157

---

*Printing and binding:
Printer Industria Gráfica S.A., Barcelona
Separations: Colour Systems Ltd, London
Paper: Condat, France*